D1587240

Joined-Up Thinking

Joined-Up Thinking

HOW TO CONNECT EVERYTHING TO EVERYTHING ELSE

Stevyn Colgan

MACMILLAN

First published 2008 by Macmillan
an imprint of Pan Macmillan Ltd
Pan Macmillan, 20 New Wharf Road, London N1 9RR
Basingstoke and Oxford
Associated companies throughout the world
www.panmacmillan.com

ISBN 978-0-230-71220-1

1 3 5 7 9 8 6 4 2

A CIP catalogue record for this book is available
from the British Library.

Typeset by SetSystems Ltd, Saffron Walden, Essex
Printed and bound in the UK by
CPI Mackays, Chatham ME5 8TD

http://stevyncolgan.blogspot.com

For my mother Meg and my late father Myghal.

Dedicated to the staff and pupils of the following schools:
Blackwater School, near Truro (1966–7)
St Marys, Penzance (1967)
St Pauls, Penzance (1968–71)
Parc Eglos School, Helston (1971–2)
Helston School (1972–9)

This book would have been impossible without them.

Contents

Contents

Contents

Contents

Contents

Contents

Introduction

An interesting and serendipitous thing happened to me a couple of years ago . . .

I was researching some material for a book about superstition. And, because it's such a huge subject, I was uncovering all kinds of fascinating facts. A lot of them got used in the book, but a lot more just didn't fit so, as I can never bear to throw interesting things away, I kept them. You never know when you might need an interesting and obscure fact one day – such as at a cocktail party or audience with the Queen. ('Excuse me, Your Majesty, but did you know that armadillos can catch leprosy?') Soon I had a huge compendium of interesting but completely unrelated facts. Or so I thought.

Quite by chance, I happened to notice that some of the facts did have a connection of sorts. Sometimes it was a feature that they shared, such as a name or a physical property. Sometimes the connection was more tenuous, such as a common word root in Latin, or I'd find a 'bridging' fact that linked two otherwise disparate pieces of trivia together. I found a link between the Sex Pistols and fossil trilobites. I found that John F. Kennedy could be linked – via his sister and a type of fish – to the Crufts International Dog Show. Starfish and Coldplay had something in common, as did chickens and Murray Mints. And the mythical Hercules and a volcano on Mars could be attached to Jesus's foreskin (in a manner of speaking). Chains of facts were forming all over the place. But then suddenly, and quite to my surprise, chains started to attach themselves to other chains. Like molecules bonding together to make more complex substances, the chains became longer and more interconnected. They grew and they grew until something truly remarkable happened: one particular chain arrived back at its starting point, creating a perfect circle of apparently unrelated but nevertheless connected facts.

That first small circle is what became Round 3 of this book. And it got me wondering if it was just a fluke. I began sifting through my notebooks and diaries and hard drives and, suddenly, another circle started to form. And another. And another. Eureka! The walls of my study became yellow with Post-it notes as each new fact was written down and then added to the most appropriate chain, hoping to form a new Round. Soon, I had ten Rounds. Then twenty. Then thirty. And all of a sudden, I had a book's worth.

Then I noticed that not only did these Rounds contain facts that could be connected together, they also contained facts that connected to facts in other Rounds . . . so even the Rounds were interconnected! I had a sudden epiphany:

Everything in the world can be connected to everything else.

For many years, we have known about something called *six degrees of separation*; the idea that every person on this planet can be linked by a chain of just six, or fewer, individuals. For example, my best mate is a guy called Huw Williams. Huw's cousin is Nicky Wire of the Manic Street Preachers. So I'm 'connected' to Nicky Wire by a chain of just one person. And, therefore, I'm linked to Manics frontman James Dean Bradfield by a chain of just two. And how many famous people does he know? I also know a guy called John Coppinger who worked on the film *The Fifth Element*. His boss in the costume department was Jean-Paul Gaultier, who designed Madonna's iconic pointy bra for her Blonde Ambition tour ... and Madonna snogged Britney at the 2003 Video Music Awards. So there's a three-person chain of association between me and Ms Spears. Me, John, Jean-Paul, Madge, Britney. But lest you think that this is all about friends in glamorous professions, I could mention my brother-in-law Rob. He's a plumber and gas fitter ... but he was once Ozzy Osbourne's plumber and gas fitter. And because Ozzy's married to Sharon, I'm linked to Simon Cowell by just three people. So maybe I shouldn't have been surprised when I found that I could do the same thing with facts; a kind of six degrees of *information*.

I hope you enjoy this series of cyclic journeys through the land of trivia. I have tried to ensure that all of the facts in this book are actually factual. However, as comedian and writer David Mitchell once said, 'If I knew how I knew everything I knew then I'd only be able to know half as much because it would all be clogged up with where I knew it from.'[1] I can't always cite the origins of some of these facts, but I've

---

1 Heard on the BBC quiz show *Would I Lie to You?* broadcast on 23 June 2007.

checked and rechecked them (as far as possible) and I'm pretty confident that the vast majority are correct.

Don't beat me up if one or two are wrong.

Just enjoy the journey.

Round 1

THE DARK SIDE
OF THE RAINBOW

Seven is a number steeped in lore and superstition. Certainly, Sir Isaac Newton (1642–1727), who spent more of his life studying alchemy than he did science, believed in the law of sevens; the idea that the natural laws of the universe obeyed a simple mystical numerical rule. After all, in Newton's time there were seven known celestial bodies other than the Earth: the Sun, Moon, Mercury, Venus, Mars, Jupiter and Saturn. There were seven metals used in alchemy: gold, silver, copper, mercury, lead, tin and iron. There are seven notes in a musical scale (A to G) and seven days in a week. There were seven levels of heaven and hundreds of references to the number seven in the Bible (a staggering 55 just in the Book of Revelation). So when Newton first split white light using a prism he naturally expected to see seven colours and must have been both confused and a bit miffed when, instead, he saw six. Certainly, he was shaken enough to have taken the unorthodox step of actually inventing a colour to make the numbers up. He called his colour indigo.

We know this because Newton recorded his actions and findings in his 1704 book *Opticks*. These days, many respectable scientists, including the late Isaac Asimov, have dismissed the colour altogether as just a shade of violet.

Curiously, the front cover of Pink Floyd's 1973 LP *Dark Side of the Moon* features a beam of light being split by a prism into only six colours. Which begs the question, did they know the Newton story? I'm told that they did, but that was not the reason why a colour was omitted from the final graphic. The album cover was designed by Storm Thorgerson of the Hipgnosis group and illustrated by artist George Hardie. Thorgerson claims that he missed out a colour not because of Isaac Newton but because he thought that two shades of violet would merge and lessen the impact of the rainbow against the black background. The cover was created with 1970s printing technology after all. Interestingly, the seventh colour is also absent from the revamped LP artwork on the twentieth and thirtieth anniversary editions of the album. Thorgerson has also stated that the image of the rainbow was a reference to the band's groundbreaking use of complex light shows during their live performances. But some people believe that there is another reason why it was chosen . . .

The rainbow is a major theme of MGM's classic 1939 musical *The Wizard of Oz* and some claim that the *Dark Side of the Moon* was specially written and arranged to synchronize with the film. Those who 'know' will tell you that if you start playing Pink Floyd's album on the MGM lion's third roar and watch and listen to both simultaneously, a remarkable series of coincidences occurs. For example, the film changes from sepia tone to colour upon Dorothy's arrival in Oz. This synchronizes almost exactly with the start of the track 'Money'. Then Glinda the do-goody-good witch appears at the same time as the line 'do-goody-good bullshit' is sung. And during the guitar solo the Munchkins' dance routine seems to follow the various tempo changes and the soldiers also appear to be marching in time with the music. Watch the two together and make up your own mind. The film is much longer than the album, of course, but aficionados will tell you that you have to play the album three times through. They claim that the synchronizations still occur on all three playings.[2]

For the filming of *The Wizard of Oz*, dwarfs were flown in from all over the world to play the Munchkins. They were kept segregated from the other actors during the making of the film and rumours went around Hollywood of wild orgies, drunken debauchery and drug-taking in the dwarf trailers. It has been suggested that many of these stories were put about by an alcohol-fuelled Judy Garland and the film's producer Mervyn Le Roy. Then, allegedly, one of the Munchkins developed a crush on Garland, and when he found his love unrequited, hanged himself as the cameras rolled – his body can be seen swinging from a tree at the end of the Tin Man's scene. Of course, it's just an urban myth ... or so claim MGM. They say that the shadowy figure was probably a stagehand accidentally on set or, more likely, a flamingo, stork or pelican. The studio had hired several large birds from the Los Angeles Zoo to add realism to the scenes. But watch the scene and judge for yourself – if you don't own the film, the clip appears several times on

---

2 You can download a full script following all three plays at Shawn Hare's Dark Side of the Rainbow website at: http://members.cox.net/stegokitty/ dsotr_pages/dsotr.htm.

YouTube. The alleged suicidee is in the distance at top left of screen.

Despite the 'hanging Munchkin' story being almost certainly untrue, the myth has persisted and was recently turned into a stage play called *Babylon Heights* by Dean Kavanagh and *Trainspotting* author Irvine Welsh. The play opened to condemnation from dwarfs everywhere, mainly because the show's producers chose to cast the play with 'normal'-sized actors working with outsized sets and props. The Restricted Growth Association said, 'This is just another example of the media ridiculing the lives of people of restricted growth, who are already disadvantaged. It's disappointing that theatre needs, for the sake of entertainment, to be disrespectful and irresponsible. If you changed the references to people in wheelchairs, this wouldn't be allowed. Why is it allowed with people of restricted growth?' However, writing in the *Guardian* newspaper, Welsh was keen to refute this, claiming, 'We decided we didn't want to have a situation whereby sensationalist elements of the media might portray the experience as a bunch of "normal-sized" people sitting in a theatre watching "dwarfs" perform ... The play resolutely attacks the spirit of discrimination, including the type actively practised by the studio at the time. It does this not by painting the characters as perfect and virtuous, but by making them real people.'[3]

'People of restricted growth' is the preferred term because of the negative connotations attached to 'dwarf' and 'midget'. Most of those negative connotations come from the world of fairy tales and mythology where dwarfs, and little people of all types from trolls and Cornish piskies to elves and leprechauns, are generally portrayed as mischievous and occasionally downright nasty. One exception to this can be found in *Snow White and the Seven Dwarfs*. These chaps are quite friendly and, depending on which version you read, were woodcutters, miners or hunters. We are most familiar with the characters from Walt Disney's 1937 animated film, Doc, Sleepy, Happy, Grumpy, Bashful, Sneezy and Dopey, but woe betide you if you use those characters in your pantomime, play or school fete as the famously litigious Disney corporation lawyers are liable to spring to animated life. Before Disney's film, the dwarfs (or should it be 'dwarves'?)[4]

---

3 *Guardian*, Thursday 20 July 2006.

4 Debate still rages over which is correct. Dwarfs would seem to be the academics' choice – for example, astronomers say dwarfs when referring to dwarf stars. There was a story that J.R.R. Tolkein invented 'dwarves' so

were best known from a 1912 Broadway play of the same name by Winthrop Ames. In this version, they were called Blick, Flick, Snick, Glick, Plick, Whick and Quee. Before that came the Grimm Brothers version of an old German story (which, in turn, may have originated in Asia), and in these older tales the dwarfs were not named at all. However, the one element that is constant across all of these different versions is that there are always seven little men.

Seven is a number that turns up time and time again in popular culture: *The Magnificent Seven*, *Seven Deadly Sins*, *Seven Samurai*, *Blake's Seven*, the seven seas, *Seven Brides for Seven Brothers* ... The list goes on and on. It appears in the beliefs of most major religions. We've already mentioned its many occurrences in the Bible but it's also a major symbolic number for Muslims. During the hajj, for example, devotees walk seven times around the Kaaba in Mecca. Buddha is often depicted sitting within the seven petals of the lotus flower. The Jewish Talmud refers to the seven commandments which comprise the universal moral code as *Sheva mizvot bnei Noah* (the seven

***

that the race sounded equal and similar to elves (not elfs). But there are nineteenth-century appearances of 'dwarves' ... and even an alternative plural 'dwarrows'. Discuss.

commandments of the sons of Noah). If folklore is to be believed, a seventh son of a seventh son is destined to have extraordinary powers. The Pythagoreans called seven the perfect number as it is the total number of sides in a triangle and a square, the perfect geometric figures. In early medicine doctors noted that there are seven orifices in the body: the ears, nostrils, mouth, anus and urethra. In Jaques' famous soliloquy from *As You Like It*, Shakespeare tells us all about the seven ages of man – infancy, childhood, the lover, the soldier, the justice, old age, dementia (and death):

> *All the world's a stage,*
> *And all the men and women merely players:*
> *They have their exits and their entrances;*[5]
> *And one man in his time plays many parts,*
> *His acts being seven ages.*

And on 7 July 1977 (7/7/77) all sorts of weird and wonderful things happened. A lady called Elizabeth Severn of Yorkshire turned 77 years old, and a child was born in Adelaide, Australia at 7.07 a.m. whose birth weight was 7 pounds 7 ounces. Meanwhile, in

---

5 Seven of them in fact . . . Sorry.

London, the Stock Exchange at lunchtime was 7.7 points down and the temperature reached a high of 77 degrees Fahrenheit. Australia were 77 days into their cricket tour when, in the seventy-seventh over, Walters took his score to 77, to the delight of partner Marsh who was batting at number seven.

And guess what the most popular day for marriages was in 2007? The seventh of July of course. More than three times as many weddings took place on that day than is usual for early July because seven is considered lucky in Western culture.

Seven is a number steeped in lore and super-stition . . .

NEVER MIND
THE FOSSILS

The word petroleum derives from the Greek word *petra* (meaning rock) and the Latin *oleum* (meaning oil). From *petra* we get such words as petrified (literally, turned to stone), petroglyph (a carving or line drawing on rock, often prehistoric) and petrochemical.

Petra is an archaeological site in south-west Jordan. First revealed to the Western world by Swiss explorer Johann Ludwig Burckhardt in 1812, the 2000-year-old site features extraordinary buildings and structures carved into the red rock by a civilization called the Nabataeans. Despite the age of the settlement, Petra is a relatively modern name. Originally, the site was called Rekem and is mentioned in the Dead Sea Scrolls. Petra is featured in *Indiana Jones and the Last Crusade* as the temple in which Indiana finds the Holy Grail.

Petra was also the name of the first *Blue Peter* pet.

Blue Peter's fiftieth birthday took place on Thursday 16 October 2008, and during the programme's long history it has had many presenters and a number of pets. Although they belong to the show, some live at home with the presenters. The first of these was Petra, a female mongrel, who made her maiden appearance on the show in 1962. It was also her only appearance. It was only revealed in the 1990s that Petra did in fact die after that first show. (As far as I can tell, the cause is unknown.) To avoid upsetting the programme's young viewers, producer Biddy Baxter found a similar-looking replacement puppy and no one was any the wiser for 30 years. Petra Mark II stayed with the show until 1977 and had a number of puppies of her own, including Patch, who also became a *Blue Peter* pet.[6]

The show takes its name from an international maritime signalling flag. The Blue Peter is a dark blue square with a smaller white square set centrally within.

---

6 This was not the last *Blue Peter* 'deception'. In 1991 Bonnie the golden retriever had puppies and viewers were asked to vote for a name. One strong contender was Biddy, but in deference to the show's producer, it was called Millie instead. And in 2007 viewers voted for a kitten to be called Cookie. BBC staff chose Socks instead but claimed it was the viewers' choice. When the deception was exposed, the current producer resigned.

If hoisted from a ship in harbour it means, 'All aboard, we're about to set sail.' However, if hoisted at sea by a fishing vessel it means, 'Bugger, my nets have got caught on something.'[7]

Nautical references abound on the show. The programme's logo is a stylized sailing ship (most commonly seen on the much-coveted *Blue Peter* badges awarded to children who have achieved something special) designed by TV artist Tony Hart. And the theme music is an old sea shanty called 'Barnacle Bill'. Over the years it has been arranged by a number of musicians including film composer David Arnold, the performers from the West End show *Stomp* and composer and multi-instrumentalist Mike Oldfield.

Mike Oldfield's *Tubular Bells* was the first ever release on Richard Branson's Virgin record label. It featured Oldfield playing over 20 different instruments taped one on top of the other, a groundbreaking technique in 1973 when everything had to be recorded onto magnetic tape and then physically cut and spliced together. Oldfield made more than 2300 recordings before he was happy. *Tubular Bells* went on to eventu-

---

7 True.

ally sell more than 13 million copies and became the eleventh-best-selling album ever released in Britain.

Oldfield had spent many months trying to get people interested in his project but no other company at the time would touch such an avant-garde project. Virgin, however, seemed to go out of its way to sign controversial or seemingly non-commercial bands, including so-called Krautrock bands like Faust and, in the late 1970s, seminal punk rockers the Sex Pistols. Oldfield became openly critical of this policy, believing that more advertising and marketing was being assigned to new 'shock' acts rather than now-established artists like himself. His song 'Punkadiddle' on the *Platinum* album (1979) is thought by many to be an attack on Virgin founder Richard Branson. A rift had already developed between the two men before *Platinum* was released and came to a head during recording of the album *Amarok* (1990), in which Oldfield embedded a secret message. Around 48 minutes into the piece there is a theme which, when read in Morse code, spells out F*ck off RB. Oldfield is still a successful recording artist today whereas the Sex Pistols, one of the punk bands that Oldfield disliked, had a controversial but very brief career.

The Sex Pistols grew out of a band originally called

the Swankers. By early 1975 the band had taken to hanging around SEX, a boutique run by Malcolm McClaren and Vivienne Westwood on the Kings Road, Chelsea. When John Lydon (aka Johnny Rotten) walked in wearing a home-made 'I Hate Pink Floyd' T-shirt, he was asked to join the band. McLaren became the group's manager and changed its name to the deliberately controversial Sex Pistols. They were signed by EMI and a first single, 'Anarchy in the UK', was released. This led to the now-famous interview with inebriated presenter Bill Grundy where he flirted with the female members of the Bromley Contingent – the Pistols' fan gang – and goaded the band into swearing on live TV. 'Bill Grundy was a dreadful drunk – I have learnt a lot from him,' said John Lydon in later interviews. 'He was a bumhole.'

Ironically, the appearance was pure chance – the band Queen had pulled out of the interview due to illness and the Pistols were a last-minute replacement. History could have been so different . . .

The tabloids had a feeding frenzy and the *Daily Mirror* ran its now legendary THE FILTH AND THE FURY headline, which became so linked to the band that it became the title of Julien Temple's 2000 rocku-mentary. A tour followed which was beset by protests, cancellations and chaos. EMI dropped the band like a hot brick.

Bass player Glen Matlock left shortly afterwards and was replaced by the barely competent John Ritchie. Rotten nicknamed him Sid Vicious after his own pet hamster, which had a habit of biting people. Don't you just love the idea of Johnny Rotten having a pet hamster? The band then signed to A&M Records and celebrated with a party at the A&M offices during which they trashed the place and threw up on the managing director's desk. The company dumped the Pistols within a week.

They were then picked up by Virgin and released their second single, 'God Save the Queen'. The single caused a huge public outcry (1977 was Queen Elizabeth's Silver Jubilee year) and was quickly banned from airplay by the BBC. Despite this, it got to number two in the charts. Many claim that it was the best-selling single in the UK for several weeks but that the industry manipulated the figures to keep the Pistols off the top. An album followed, *Never Mind the Bollocks*, which put the Pistols firmly back in the eye of the storm. A record shop in Nottingham was threatened with prosecution for displaying the album's 'obscene' cover. The case was dropped when linguistics experts satisfied judges that bollocks is a legitimate Old English term for a priest, and, anyway, the word was being used to mean nonsense rather than testicles. Curiously, the *Blue Peter* theme 'Barnacle Bill' is based upon an earlier bawdy song called 'Bollocky Bill the Sailor' which in turn is based upon an old folk song called 'Abraham Brown'.

The last ever Sex Pistols gig (not counting the comeback tours of the past few years) was at the Winterland Ballroom in San Francisco on 14 January 1978. Rotten quit after the show, famously asking the audience 'Ever get the feeling you've been cheated?' before leaving the stage. In October Sid Vicious was arrested over the alleged murder of his girlfriend Nancy Spungen. Shortly afterwards, he was found dead of a heroin overdose. His death is considered by many to be the result of a death pact with Nancy.

In 1997, in a somewhat bizarre tribute, palaeontologists Jonathan Adrain and Gregory Edgecombe named a series of fossil trilobite species after the Sex Pistols: *Arcticalymene rotteni*, *A. viciousi*, *A. jonesi*, *A. cooki* and *A. matlocki*.

Fossils are formed when the body of a dead animal or plant is covered in layers of sediment that hardens over time. The organic matter trapped within decays, leaving a void like a mould. Over many years the sediment eventually solidifies into rock. Minerals dissolved in water trickle down through this rock, filling the void left behind by the dead animal or plant. This then hardens, forming an often perfect cast of the original life form. This is, however, a very rare occurrence. Therefore the fossil record can only ever be a tiny and random sample of the billions of different creatures and plants that have inhabited the Earth in its history. The vast majority of living things have instead broken down into their constituent organic ingredients.

When organisms die and their tissues fall into anoxic water (where no oxygen is present) and are subjected to pressure, heat is created and the matter metamorphoses into a waxy substance called kerogen. When heated, kerogen transforms into hydrocarbons which, being lighter than rock or water, work their way upwards through adjacent rock layers until they become trapped beneath a layer of impermeable rock. This then forms a reservoir. As the reservoir becomes more concentrated, the massed hydrocarbons become an oil field. This can then be extracted by drilling and pumping. It is from this raw or 'crude' oil that petroleum is created.

The word petroleum derives from the Greek word *petra* (meaning rock) and . . .

CHICKENFEED

In 1885 Vincent M. Holt wrote a little book with the magnificent title *Why Not Eat Insects?*[8] In the book he makes a convincing argument for eating invertebrates and even includes recipes and suggested menus. Who could not resist the lure of *Boeuf aux chenilles* (braised beef with caterpillars), *Larves de guepes frites au rayon* (wasp grubs fried in the comb) or the ultimate supper dish *Phalenes au parmesan* (moths on toast)? But, as he points out, people in the UK have a strange and illogical prejudice against eating invertebrates that live on land. We eat prawns and crabs and oysters and cockles, but we won't eat locusts, woodlice, snails or slugs even though they are essentially the same creatures. The snails they eat in

---

8 Originally published by the British Museum (Natural History) but now reprinted by Pryor Books (1992). An online edition can be found at www.foodreference.com/html/artinsectso.html.

France are the same as our common garden snails; they're just bred to be larger and juicier. Oh, and kept well away from poisonous slug pellets.

Snails feature on the menu of the multi-award-winning Fat Duck restaurant in Bray, Berkshire. It has three Michelin stars and was Michelin restaurant of the year in 2001. It was voted best restaurant in the world in 2005 by *Restaurant* magazine. All of which surprises many people because owner and experimental head chef Heston Blumenthal delights in presenting the kind of menus that most restaurants would shy away from. On the current Tasting Menu (£125) you can enjoy the delights of snail porridge, oak moss and truffle toast, blackcurrant and green peppercorn jelly, nitro-scrambled egg and bacon ice cream, mango and Douglas Fir purée, and quail jelly with langoustine and roast foie gras.

Foie gras is a controversial luxury food made from the fattened liver of a duck (or Fat Duck, if you prefer) or, occasionally goose, that has been deliberately overfed. Many people believe that the production of foie gras should be banned as it involves unnecessary cruelty to the animals, which are force-fed. This can result in livers swollen to many times their normal size, impaired liver function, difficulty in walking and ultimately death. Force-feeding, *gavage*, is banned in many countries including the UK and USA although the resulting foodstuff isn't.

An early version of foie gras was being produced as early as 2500 BC by the ancient Egyptians and there is a bas relief (petroglyph) on the wall of the tomb of Mereruka in the necropolis of Saqqara, showing the practice taking place. *Gavage* then spread across to the Mediterranean and Pliny the Elder recorded in his *Natural History* that Roman gastronome Marcus Gavius Apicius would make what was called *iecur ficatum* ('figged liver') by 'cramming [geese] with dried figs, and when they are fat enough, they are drenched with wine mixed with honey, and immediately killed'. The incredibly strange Roman emperor Elagabalus or Heliogabalus (AD 203–22) is said to have fed his dogs on foie gras, which can't have been the best thing for their health. Mind you, he also invented a new chief god (called Deus Sol Invictus) to replace Jupiter, had himself circumcised so that he could elect himself high priest, forced his senators to watch as he danced around the temple to the sound of drums and cymbals, wore women's clothes and make-up, and prostituted himself in taverns and brothels. Not surprisingly perhaps he was killed during a military coup by the Praetorian Guard.

The literal translation of foie gras is 'fat liver'. Mardi Gras translates as 'fat Tuesday'. Mardi Gras gets its name from the tradition of having a big feast to use up all the forbidden foods before entering Lent.

The Tuesday before Lent, which starts on Ash Wednesday, is known as Shrove Tuesday. It is a day of penitence, a day to be shrived. Shriving is where a person confesses their sins and receives absolution for them. Shrove Tuesday is also the day to rid the house of all luxury foods like eggs, fats and sugars. An easy and popular recipe for using up these ingredients is pancakes, which is why Shrove Tuesday in the UK is not Mardi Gras but Pancake Day.

The day is marked with church services, the eating of pancakes and pancake races. The races are said to have originated in the village of Olney, near Milton Keynes in Buckinghamshire. The story goes that back in 1445 a woman lost track of the time on Shrove Tuesday, and was still cooking pancakes when the church bells began to toll, calling the faithful to confession. In her panic, she ran to the church still wearing her apron and carrying her frying pan. Since

1948 the event has been re-enacted in Olney every year with a 415-yard race from Market Place to halfway down Church Lane. The tradition was resurrected by Canon Ronald Collins, who came across references and photographs of such events taking place in the nineteenth and early-twentieth centuries. An almost identical race takes place on the same day in the town of Liberal in Kansas, USA. The Americans decided to challenge Olney after reading about the event in *Time* magazine in 1950. And the rivalry has gone on ever since. The races are only open to women aged 18 or over and they have to live in either Olney or Liberal. Pancakes are tossed by all of the competitors at the start of the race and the winner is required to toss her pancake again at the finish. The pancakes are carried throughout the race in a frying pan.

The world's largest frying pan was produced by Mumford Sheet Metal Works in Selbyville, Delaware, USA in 1950. It was ten feet in diameter and was made for the annual Delmarva Chicken Festival hosted by Delmarva Poultry Inc. It was used every year until 1998, when it was retired and put on display in a museum. It had cooked over a hundred tons of chicken.

With a population of more than 24 billion – three

billion in China alone until the recent bird flu epidemic – there are more chickens in the world than any other type of bird. If all the chickens eaten worldwide in a year by just Kentucky Fried Chicken consumers were laid end to end, they would circle the Earth eleven times, or make a line of chickens from the Earth to the Moon and a further 50,000 miles beyond.

On 10 September 1945 Utah chicken keeper Lloyd Olsen chose a white Wyandotte for his lunch and, armed with a sharp axe, set out to give the bird a humane and quick death. But, amazingly, despite apparently losing its head, the bird continued to act just like any other chicken. Olsen decided that if Mike, as the chicken was called, had that much will to live, he would figure out a way to feed and water him.

Olsen took Mike to the University of Utah in Salt Lake City in an effort to find out why the chicken still lived. It was decided that the axe had missed the jugular vein and a clot had prevented Mike from bleeding to death. And although most of Mike's head had been removed, enough of the brain stem remained to keep the bird's autonomic system going. Olsen fed the chicken using an eye-dropper and had him regularly checked by vets and animal welfare groups. They always found him to be in good health, all things considered.

Mike 'the headless wonder chicken' became a celebrity. He was insured to the tune of $10,000 and appeared in both *Life* and *Time* magazines. Amazingly, he survived for 18 months after his decapitation and, to the surprise of all, seemed to be as happy and content as any other chicken.

As adults, chickens are mostly vegetarian and are fed with a mix of corn, soybean meal, seeds and ground oyster shells – this last provides calcium for making egg shells. Up until the age of about two months, however, the growing chicks are carnivorous, preferring earthworms and mealworms.

Mealworms are the larvae of the darkling beetle (genus Tenebrionidae). They are vermicious (worm-like) in appearance and have a hardened skin suitable for burrowing through soil and leaf litter. They are an incredibly rich source of nutrition, having more complete protein than soy, meat, or fish and are concentrated sources of calcium, niacin, magnesium, potassium, the B vitamins and many other nutrients. Many of the world's famine problems could be solved by utilizing the extraordinary nutritional value of these insects. And, indeed, many other types of invertebrate. For example, 3.5 ounces of crickets or grasshoppers contain 121 calories, 0.4 ounces of protein, 0.2 ounces of fat, 0.17 ounces of carbohydrates, 0.02 ounces of calcium, 0.006 ounces of phosphorous, 0.03 ounces of iron, 0.001 ounces of thiamin, 0.003 ounces of riboflavin and 0.01 ounces of niacin. Sadly, however, the actions of well-meaning Christian missionaries in the 1800s persuaded many of the world's poorest and hungriest people that eating bugs is 'icky', a belief that persists for most of us to the present day, which is a tragic shame as there are 1,462 recorded species of edible insect and there are enough of them out there to solve all of the world's food shortage problems.

Fully 95 per cent of all living creatures on Earth are insects – that's approximately ten quintillion (10,000,000,000,000,000,000) individual insects alive on this planet at this exact moment. Ten per cent of the total biomass of life on Earth is made up just of ants (some scientists claim the figure may even be as high as 15–20 per cent). And that's not counting the other arthropods – spiders, scorpions, crabs, lobsters, woodlice, etc., many of which are also edible. By comparison, we humans make up just 0.33 per cent, and there are six billion of us. So there are plenty of insects to go around as long as we can get over our prejudices about using them as food.

In 1885, Vincent M. Holt wrote a little book with the magnificent title of *Why Not Eat Insects?* . . .

THE SIX DEGREES
OF RICK WAKEMAN

The piano on the David Bowie hit 'Life on Mars?' was played by Yes keyboard wizard and TV personality Rick Wakeman when he was a session musician (he also played keyboards on many other hit singles including Cat Stevens' 'Morning Has Broken').

Many people believe that David Bowie has different-coloured eyes. He hasn't. As a result of a childhood fight with his friend George Underwood, he suffered an eye injury that left one pupil permanently dilated. It therefore looks darker than the other.

George Underwood remained a close friend and went on to be a successful artist and designer, producing several of Bowie's best-known album covers including those for *The Rise and Fall of Ziggy Stardust* and *Hunky Dory*, which featured the single 'Life on Mars?' with

Rick Wakeman on piano. Underwood has also illustrated a large number of book covers. Among them was Richard Matheson's *What Dreams May Come*, which was turned into a Hollywood film in 1998 by director Vincent Ward. The film's star was manic stand-up comedian and Oscar-winning actor Robin Williams.

Robin Williams played Osric in Kenneth Branagh's film version of *Hamlet*, a role made famous on the stage by Sir Alec Guinness (playing opposite Sir John Geilgud's Hamlet). Sir Alec Guinness, of course, played the older Obi-Wan Kenobi in George Lucas's *Star Wars* films. The younger Obi-Wan was played by Scottish actor Ewan McGregor, who appeared with Robin Williams in the animated film *Robots* (2005) and in *Being Human* (1993).

In *Being Human*, a comedy drama set across several thousand years of history, McGregor played the bit part of Alvaraz. Another bit part – that of a prehistoric shaman – was played by Robert Carlyle. The two of them had previously appeared in the film of Irvine Walsh's blackly comic *Trainspotting*. This was directed by Danny Boyle, who made a short film in 2002 called *Alien Love Triangle* starring Kenneth Branagh . . . who made the film version of *Hamlet*, which starred Robin Williams as Osric.

Osric: A Missionary Tale is an epic poem written by
Charlotte Elizabeth (1790–1846). It is very nearly
24,000 words long. Charlotte Elizabeth Tonna, to give
her full name, was an evangelical Protestant poet and
author whose work was sufficiently anti-Catholic to
have been placed on the Vatican's *Index Expurgatorium*.
The *Expurgatorium* was a list of amendments to be
made to books before they would be accepted by
Rome as suitable for Catholics to read. Those that
could not be corrected were placed on the *Index
Librorum Prohibitorum* (List of Prohibited Books).
Charlotte Elizabeth became deaf at the age of ten and
developed an interest in teaching deaf children as a
result. She was married twice: firstly to Captain George
Phelan of the 60th Regiment (the King's Royal Rifle
Corps, until recently known as the Royal Green Jack-
ets and since 2007 simply as The Rifles) and then to
Lewis Hippolytus Joseph Tonna, a religious writer 22
years her junior.

Hippolytus is a curious choice of name as he wasn't
exactly the most inspiring or heroic of Greek mythological characters. His stepmother Phaedra took a
fancy to him, but when he spurned her advances, she
told her husband – Hippolytus' dad Theseus – that her
stepson had raped her. Theseus therefore did what any

outraged husband would do: he arranged with the sea god Poseidon for a sea monster to frighten his son's horses and they dragged him to his death. The whole sad, sorry tale is made even more bizarre by the fact that Theseus was also supposedly one of Poseidon's many children, making the sea god Hippolytus' grandfather.

Poseidon certainly sowed his wild oats with gusto. In the Greek myths he sired 58 children by at least 27 different women. He wasn't too picky either; one of his conquests was the snake-headed Gorgon, Medusa. Poseidon – known as Neptune to the Romans – was a son of the Titans Chronos and Rhea. At one point, for reasons which will become clear in a later Round, Chronos ate all of his children. Only Zeus and Poseidon escaped, the latter by feeding a small horse to his dad instead.

Poseidon was not only the god of the sea but also of horses and earthquakes. If he was appeased, he would calm the oceans, create new islands and save ships from sinking. Sailors would drown horses as a sacrifice to him. But if he was offended or ignored, he would bash his three-pronged trident on the ground, creating earthquakes and shipwrecks.

One very famous fictional shipwreck was named

after him. *The Poseidon Adventure* (1969) was a novel by Paul Gallico and spawned a film in 1972, a film sequel, *Beyond the Poseidon Adventure*, in 1979, a TV movie in 2005 and a cinema remake, *Poseidon*, in 2006. The story takes place aboard a luxury ocean liner overturned by a tidal wave. The passengers and crew then have to find their way out through the upside-down ship.

Disaster also struck the real *Poseidon*. HMS *Poseidon*, a Parthian-class British submarine, sank following a collision with a Chinese freighter in 1931. Thirty of the crew managed to get out of the vessel before it reached the seabed. However, the remainder were trapped on the ocean floor, 130 feet down. Eight attempted to escape of which two failed to reach the surface in time and a third died later. Twenty-two men died in total.

Until the *Poseidon* incident, standard procedure was to 'go down with the submarine' and await rescue. However, the successful escape of 30 crew as it sank prompted a change in policy. From this point on, the Admiralty advised that crew should attempt to escape at the earliest opportunity.

The Admiralty is the governing body of the Royal Navy. It was formed in 1546 by King Henry VIII and is the oldest branch of the Ministry of Defence. The MoD is an amalgam of five departments of state: the Admiralty, the War Office, the Air Ministry, the Ministry of Aviation and the original Ministry of Defence. The five departments came together in 1971.

1971 was the year that David Bowie released his *Hunky Dory* album. It spawned several singles including 'Oh You Pretty Things', 'Changes', 'Queen Bitch' and the anthemic 'Life on Mars?'. Rick Wakeman played piano on that track and on the entire album. Did I mention that already? Many people have noted the similarity of 'Life on Mars?' to 'My Way', one of the world's most popular songs.

'My Way' has identical chords and the same grand Broadway feeling as 'Life on Mars?' but this is more than just a coincidence. In 1968 Bowie wrote some English lyrics for a French song called *'Comme d'habitude'*. He called this new song 'Even a Fool Learns to Love'. But then the rights to *'Comme d'habitude'* were bought by Canadian songwriter Paul Anka . . . who then rewrote it and called it 'My Way'. It has since been recorded by many artists, among them Pavarotti, Shane MacGowan, Elvis Presley and Sid Vicious, but most famously by Frank Sinatra, for whom it became a signature song.

Bowie's 'Life On Mars?' was recorded as a deliberate Sinatra parody in annoyance at having missed out on a fortune. A cheeky sleeve note on the album states the song was 'inspired by Frankie'. The song had to wait until 1973 for a single release because *Hunky Dory* had not been enough of a commercial success initially.

The piano on the David Bowie hit 'Life on Mars?' was played by . . .

I'D RATHER HAVE A FULL BOTTLE IN FRONT OF ME . . .

Crufts is the largest dog show in the world (as attested to in the *Guinness Book of Records*). The 2007 show saw more than 20,000 dogs and 178 different breeds from 32 different countries enter the various competitions. The competition is organized by the Kennel Club of Great Britain and takes its name from its founder, dog expert Charles Cruft (1852–1938), who started the show in 1886.

In 1987 the award of Crufts Best in Show was won by an Afghan hound called CH Viscount Grant owned by Mr and Mrs Chris Amoo. Chris Amoo was the lead singer of 1970s band The Real Thing. They had a number of Top Ten singles including 'You to Me Are Everything', 'Can't Get by Without You' and 'Can

You feel the Force?'. The band got their first break on the UK talent show *Opportunity Knocks* in the early 1970s. This was a show that launched the careers of many entertainers including Frank Carson, Les Dawson, Little and Large and Lena Zavaroni.

Zavaroni wasn't quite 11 years old when she first appeared on the show in 1974. Her powerful voice (reminiscent of past child prodigies like Judy Garland and Shirley Temple) so impressed the public that they voted her the winner for an unparalleled five weeks in a row. Her first single, 'Mama, He's Making Eyes at Me', made her the youngest person ever to have a Top Ten hit and the youngest person to ever appear on *Top of the Pops*. In a meteoric rise to fame, she sang with Frank Sinatra, Liza Minnelli and Lucille Ball, performed at the White House for President Gerald Ford, appeared on countless TV shows and the Royal Variety Show and had her own TV series . . . and all before she was 17.

However, the pressures of stardom at such a young age affected her badly. She developed anorexia nervosa at the age of 13 and it stayed with her throughout her life. At one point her weight dropped to four stone. As if this were not enough to cope with, her marriage collapsed, her mother died of a tranquillizer overdose in 1989 and a house fire destroyed all of her showbiz memorabilia. Her lowest ebb came in 1999 when she was accused of stealing a 50p packet of jelly from a convenience store. By this time she was suffering with depression (she'd made one suicide attempt) and was living in a council house in Hertfordshire and surviving on £48.80 weekly state benefit. In a final attempt to beat the anorexia that was destroying her life, she was admitted to the University Hospital of Wales in Cardiff for a controversial brain operation. Sadly, she contracted pneumonia after the operation and was too weak to beat it. She died on 1 October 1999 aged just 35.

The brain operation she had decided to undergo is called a leucotomy. It is also known as a prefrontal lobotomy. This severs the frontal lobe of the brain from its underlying structures. Between 1939 and 1951 more than 18,000 lobotomies were performed in the United States alone. It was widely used to control undesirable behaviour – and widely misused to treat 'insane' prisoners. Results proved less than satisfactory. While some patients were happier and more emotionally stable, a large number were left feeling dull and apathetic. The procedure fell into disrepute and it is a very rare operation these days. It has been successfully replaced with the use of psychotropic drugs.

Rose-Marie Kennedy, the younger sister of John F. Kennedy, underwent a lobotomy at the age of 23 in an attempt to cure her violent mood swings and depression. But after the operation she had a child-like mentality, was incontinent and would stare blankly at walls for hours. Her speech became nothing more than meaningless babble.

Rose-Marie died in hospital in 2005, the first (and so far only) of the nine Kennedy siblings to die of natural causes. Brother Joseph died in action in World War II; John was assassinated while president of the USA; Robert (Bobby) was assassinated while running for the presidency; and Kathleen was killed in a plane crash. Ted, Patricia, Jean and Eunice are still with us at the time of writing . . . but must be a bit worried.

Rose-Marie's experience inspired her sister Eunice to found the Special Olympics in 1962. In recognition of this, Eunice is the only woman (to date) to have ever appeared on a US coin except Lady Liberty. The coin was the commemorative 1995 Special Olympics Silver Dollar.

The silver dollar or characin is a small fish belonging to the family *Characidae*. They come from Central and South America and are a popular tropical fish to keep in home and public aquaria.

The Royal Aquarium (and Imperial Theatre), Westminster was a public aquarium built in London in 1876 and stood on the site now occupied by Central Hall, opposite Westminster Abbey. It was built as a pleasure palace and theatre and was part-owned by Arthur Sullivan of Gilbert and Sullivan fame. Its licence to operate as a theatre was often at risk because of the dangerous and sensational acts that appeared there, such as Leotard the trapeze artist (after whom the skintight garment was named) and Zazel the lady human cannonball. What was most notable about the aquarium, however, was the number of technical problems it had maintaining the tanks in a healthy state. One popular guidebook described it thus: 'This popular place of amusement belies its name, for it has but a beggarly show of fish.'[9]

The aquarium and theatre closed and was demolished in 1903. During its short history it was a favourite venue for animal acts and shows, such as Nat

9 *The Queen's London: a Pictorial and Descriptive Record of the Streets, Buildings, Parks and Scenery of the Great Metropolis in the 59th year of the reign of Her Majesty Queen Victoria* (1896), Cassell and Co. Ltd, London.

Emmett's Wonderful Goats and Vidcou's Performing Fleas. In 1886 a young man called Charles Cruft took up the management of the Allied Terrier Club Show at the Royal Aquarium. Just five years later the show had grown to be a much bigger affair and had become known as Crufts.

Crufts is the largest dog show in the world . . .

YOU ONLY LIVE TWICE (UNLESS YOU'RE A TIME LORD)

In the James Bond novel *You Only Live Twice* we learn that Bond's parents both died when he was 11 years old in a climbing accident in the Aiguilles Rouges, in eastern France. They are named as Andrew Bond, a Scottish representative of the Vickers armaments firm, and Monique Delacroix from the Canton de Vaud, in south-west Switzerland. Therefore, 007 is half-Scots and half-Swiss.

Swiss cheese is the common name for Emmental. It is distinguished by large thumb-sized holes. It is a difficult cheese to make and the process involves three types of bacteria. It begins with *Streptococcus thermophilis* and *lactobacillus*, which produce much of the familiar taste and texture. Then *Propionibacter shermani* feeds on the lactic acid excreted by the other two and releases carbon dioxide gas, which slowly forms in bubbles within the cheese. It is these bubbles, when sliced, that give the cheese its distinctive holes.

Swiss cheese commonly appears in *Tom and Jerry* cartoons. In fact, it seems to be the only type of cheese to feature. In the cartoon 'O Solar Miaow' (1966) Jerry lands a spaceship in the Limburger Crater on the Moon. However, there is no indication that this is anything other than a place name as the Moon, when sliced, resembles Swiss cheese. The pungent Limburger cheese is used frequently, however, in Warner Brothers' *Looney Tunes*.

Tom and Jerry was the original stage name of Simon and Garfunkel. Paul Simon adopted the stage name Jerry Landis and Art Garfunkel called himself Tom Graph. One of their first hits as Simon and Garfunkel was 'The Sound of Silence'. Paul Simon wrote the song to try to capture the feeling of national shock and dismay following the assassination of John F. Kennedy on 22 November 1963.

The first ever episode of the BBC's *Dr Who* was broadcast the day after Kennedy's assassination. There is an oft-quoted myth that the broadcast was delayed by ten minutes due to extended news coverage. However, the truth is that it was broadcast just 80 seconds late, and that was only because sports show *Grandstand* overran.

Dr Who ran from 1963 until 1989 and the lead role was played in turn by William Hartnell, Patrick Troughton, Jon Pertwee, Tom Baker, Peter Davison, Colin Baker and Sylvester McCoy. The name Sylvester means wild and *Spiritus sylvestre* (wild spirit) was the original name given to carbon dioxide (which, as we know, makes the holes in Swiss cheese) when it was discovered by Jan Baptist van Helmont. Sylvester was also the name of the cat that appeared in many of the *Looney Tunes* cartoons. His full name was Sylvester J. Pusscat Snr. The name was apparently chosen because *Felis Silvestris Catus* is the scientific name of the domestic cat. But I digress . . .

Dr Who was resurrected for a one-off TV movie starring Paul McGann in 1996. Then in 2005 the Doctor finally returned, played initially by Christopher Eccleston and now, at the time of publication, David Tennant.

During the 1971 story 'Dr Who and the Daemons', the shot of a helicopter exploding and crashing was a piece of footage 'borrowed' from the 1963 James Bond movie *From Russia with Love*. This film was loosely based (as all Bond films are) on the books by Ian Fleming.

Ian Lancaster Fleming (1908–64) was born in Mayfair, London to Valentine Fleming MP and Evelyn Ste Croix Fleming (née Rose). His cousin is actor Christopher Lee. He had several jobs, most notably as a stockbroker and as a subeditor for the Reuters news agency. However, during World War II he worked in military intelligence, where he achieved the rank of commander, and it was here that he learned all he needed in order to create as vivid a character as James Bond.

Many of Fleming's experiences were carried over into the Bond books and films. Villain Blofeld's name was based upon a chap who frequented Boodle's, Fleming's club in St James's, London, and Bond himself was named after James Bond, a leading American ornithologist and friend. In an early scene in the twentieth Bond film, *Die Another Day*, Pierce Brosnan is seen reading one of Bond's books, *Birds of the West Indies*. Fleming orchestrated Operation Goldeneye during the war, a plan to keep communication links with Gibraltar open if Spain went over to the Nazis. He later named his estate in Saint Mary Parish, Jamaica after the operation. The 1995 film of the same name was not based upon a Fleming book but was named to commemorate Fleming's involvement in the war.

In total, Fleming wrote 14 Bond books: *Casino Royale* (1953), *Live and Let Die* (1954), *Moonraker* (1955), *Diamonds Are Forever* (1956), *From Russia With Love* (1957), *Dr No* (1958), *Goldfinger* (1959), *For Your Eyes Only* (1960), *Thunderball* (1961), *The Spy Who Loved Me* (1962), *On Her Majesty's Secret Service* (1963), *You Only Live Twice* (1964), *The Man with the Golden Gun* (1965), and *Octopussy/The Living Daylights* (1966), all of which have been used as film titles. Fleming only saw the first two films (*Dr No* and *From Russia with Love*) before his death. Consequently, he never saw Roger Moore, his own choice, as Bond or his cousin Christopher Lee as Scaramanga in *The Man with the Golden Gun*. The newest film (at time of writing) is to be called *Quantum of Solace* and is based on one of Fleming's short stories.

In *You Only Live Twice* James Bond's mother is named for the first time and Fleming borrowed part of his own mother's name – Ste Croix. Bond's mother was Monique Delacroix from Switzerland. Remember?

Ferdinand Victor Eugène Delacroix (1798–1863) was an important French romantic painter whose work would later inspire the Impressionists. His most famous painting is *Liberty Leading the People* (1830) and some claim that the boy at the far right of the painting holding up a gun was the inspiration for the character Gavroche in Victor Hugo's *Les Misérables*.

In *Les Misérables* Jean Valjean's prisoner number is famously 24601. The number crops up regularly in TV series. It was Hank Jennings' prisoner number in the series *Twin Peaks* and appears regularly in *The Simpsons*. For instance, it was both Sideshow Bob's prisoner number and Principal Skinner's prisoner number in Vietnam. *Simpsons* creator Matt Groening is on record as saying that in-jokes abound on the show because it has really smart writers: 'There are jokes you won't get,' he says, 'unless you've actually attended a few classes in college.'

The number 24601 is also the zip code (postcode) for Amonate in the US State of Virginia.

Virginia was named after the so-called Virgin Queen, Elizabeth I. There are towns called Elizabeth in Colorado, Illinois, Indiana, New Jersey and Pennsylvania but, curiously, none in Virginia. Common shortenings of the name Elizabeth include: Babette, Bess, Bet, Beth, Betsie, Betta, Bettina, Betty, Eli, Eliza, Elsie, Elspeth, Ilsa, Isabel, Isabella, Libby, Lilibet,

Lilla, Lisa, Lisbet, Lisbeth, Liz, Liza, Lizzie, Tetsy, Tetty and Bessie.

Bessie was the name of the high-powered Edwardian-style car driven by the Doctor in *Dr Who*. The bright yellow roadster made its debut in the Jon Pertwee story 'Doctor Who and the Silurians' in 1970. Its number plate read WHO1 but this was not the car's real registration number as unfortunately this wasn't available. The car's actual number was MTR5 and it had to show this plate when driven on a public road.

Bessie's final regular appearance was in Tom Baker's debut story 'Robot' (1974) and, curiously, MTR5 is also a kind of robot designed and manufactured by Brooks Automation Inc. It can be fitted with a number of arms and programmed for tasks such as those found on an assembly line. Brooks Automation head offices are at 15 Elizabeth Drive, Chelmsford, Massachusetts.

Chelmsford, Essex is where the Chantry School once stood. Among its famous alumni was magician, scientist, astrologer and all-round know-it-all Dr John Dee. Dee was an adviser to . . . Queen Elizabeth I. He invented the term 'British Empire'.

Actors Sean Connery and Roger Moore are Knights of the British Empire and between them played James

Bond in thirteen movies (fourteen if you count *Never Say Never Again*[10]).

In the James Bond novel *You Only Live Twice*, we learn . . .

FRANKIE SAYS . . .
SCOOBY DOOBY DOO

The first couple ever to be shown in bed together on prime-time TV in America were Fred and Wilma Flintstone. Wilma Flintstone's maiden name was Slaghoople, although two episodes have her meeting old school friends who claim she was called Wilma Pebble. Did she marry twice? Does Fred know? Incidentally, her next-door neighbour Betty Rubble's maiden name was Betty Jean McBricker.

The show was made by legendary animation company Hanna-Barbera Productions, who also produced *Scooby Doo – Where Are You?*. While the series was being developed, Scooby had the far less interesting name of Too Much, the Scooby Gang were called the Mysteries Five and its human members named Kelly, Linda, Ronnie and WW. These were later renamed to become the characters we know today. They were also given surnames despite these being rarely, if ever, used in the series: Fred Herman Jones, Daphne Blake, Velma Dace Dinkley and Norville 'Shaggy' Rogers. The dog's full name is Scoobert 'Scooby' Doo.

Scooby Doo is a Great Dane and one of triplets, the others being Skippy Doo and Dooby Doo. In addition he has two brothers called Howdy Doo and Yabba Doo and a sister called Ruby Doo, who is the mother of his intensely irritating nephew Scrappy.

The name Scooby Doo was taken from an ad-lib by Frank Sinatra in his song 'Strangers in the Night'.

The young Frank Sinatra was depicted in many cartoons, often parodied for his stick-thin physique. He features in Warner Brothers' 1944 *Swooner Crooner*, where he is a rooster whose singing puts the hens off laying. He is also lampooned by Disney's famous yellow dog in *Pluto's Blue Note* (1947) and appears as a singing sword in the 1988 movie *Who Framed Roger Rabbit*.[11]

In *Roger Rabbit*, cartoon characters or Toons exist side by side with human beings. Toons are not bound

---

11 The title did not have a question mark because of an old superstition that films with a question mark in the title do badly at the box office.

by the normal laws of physics and bend them 'when it's funny'. They can be squashed, thrown great distances, bashed without harm and produce items impossibly out of thin air. Hammerspace is a term used by cartoon fans to denote the place from which cartoon characters can retrieve objects – apparently from nowhere. It is believed to have been coined by fans of Rumiko Takahashi's anime and manga series *Ranma ½*, where heroine Akane Tendo has the ability to summon hammers and mallets from empty air. The phenomenon is not new; way back in the 1920s Felix the Cat was pulling objects out of his magic bag that were larger than the bag itself[12]. In computer games characters frequently have a so-called magic satchel in which they store far more and larger items than is physically possible (Hermione Granger stores an entire library of books in one such satchel in the Harry Potter books), and in the live action film *The Mask* (1994) Jim Carrey plays homage to various *Looney Tunes* movies by producing a huge multi-barrelled gun, a bazooka and hundreds of items from his pockets when searched. Dr

---

12 There is a species of deep-sea hairy anglerfish (*Caulophryne polnema*) that can actually swallow prey bigger than itself. It has an enormously expandable stomach that enables it to make use of anything edible that passes by in the cold, pitch-black depths where it lives.

Who's TARDIS (and, as revealed in 2005, his coat pockets) are bigger on the inside than the outside, and in earlier 'Silver Age' (late 1950s to early 1970s) Superman comics and cartoons, the Man of Steel concealed his Clark Kent business clothes (including hat and shoes) in a pouch in the inner lining of his cape ... yet his cape never bulged or hung heavily. Hammerspace? Possibly, although in later comics there was talk of 'super-compressible anti-wrinkle material' and even that Clark had to buy new clothes every time.

Superman appears in many episodes of the TV series *Seinfeld*, but not every episode as the urban myth claims. There is a Superman fridge magnet on Jerry's fridge and a Superman figure near his hi-fi. In one episode Jerry picks the phrase Jor-El (Superman's real name) as his bank pin number[13] and in another he describes a girlfriend's house as a fortress of solitude.[14] This connection was taken one stage further in 2004 in

13 The USA is so populous that credit-card PIN numbers can be anything between four and eight digits long. The numerical keypads on the ATM machines also have three letters printed on each – just like on mobile-phone keys – and many people use these to remember their PIN. E.g. TREE could be a trigger word for the PIN 8733.

14 A full list of the references can be found at www.supermanhomepage. com/tv/tv.php?topic=articles/seinfeld.

a series of commercials for American Express featuring an animated Superman and Jerry Seinfeld.

American Express (Amex) was founded in 1850 by Henry Wells, William Fargo and John Butterfield. Wells and Fargo are most famous for their overland mail services and Wells Fargo stagecoaches featured in many Hollywood Westerns, as did Wells Fargo banks. In fact, a film was made in 1937 called *Wells Fargo*, starring Joel McCrea, Bob Burns and Frances Dee. During the making of the film assistant propman Jack Leys accidentally shot himself when he reached into the prop chest for a gun. The film was directed by Frank Lloyd.

Lloyd was one of the 36 founders of the Academy of Motion Picture Arts and Sciences (AMPAS) and was president of the academy 1934/5. AMPAS is responsible for awarding the annual Academy Awards or Oscars. The statuettes were designed by MGM art director Cedric Gibbons and sculpted by George Stanley. The figure is of a knight standing on a reel of film, hands gripping a sword. This is a crusader's sword signifying innovation and advancement, and the reel of film has five spokes representing the five original branches of the Academy (actors, directors, producers, technicians and writers). Each figure is made of 24-carat-gold-plated britannium (a high-grade form of pewter alloy), stands 13½ inches tall and weighs 8½ pounds, about the same as an average-sized new-born baby.

The name Oscar was coined in 1931 when an executive director of the Academy, Margaret Herrick, commented that the statue resembled her Uncle Oscar. We can only hope that he wasn't habitually naked and wielding a sword. Incidentally, the Emmy Awards are named after the image orthicon or immy, a camera tube used in television; Grammy is short for gramophone; the Tony is named after Broadway actress Antoinette Perry; the mystery writers' Edgar is named for Edgar Allan Poe and the Hugo is named after Hugo Gernsback, the founder of many popular science fiction magazines.

In 2002 the Oscar for best actress went to Halle Berry for her performance in *Monster's Ball*. The win surprised many people as Berry's career has been somewhat of a mixed bag and includes some truly dire films such as *Catwoman*, for which she won the 2004 Razzies Award (short for raspberries) for worst actress – to her great credit she collected it in person. She also appeared in the 1994 live-action film *The Flintstones*, playing Mr Slate's secretary Sharon Stone. The role, incidentally, was turned down by the real Sharon Stone.

The Flintstones TV series is famous for its lack of continuity. Apart from the query over Wilma's maiden name, there are many other inconsistencies. Depending upon which episode you watch, the modern stone-age family live at 301 Cobblestone Way, Bedrock 70777, or 301 Cobblestone Lane, or 345 Stonecave Road, or 222 Rocky Way. Similarly, Fred works at a quarry, which is variously called the Slaterock Gravel Company, or the Bedrock Gravel Company, or the Rockhead Quarry, or the Cave Construction Company.

The first couple ever to be shown in bed together on prime-time TV in America were Fred and Wilma Flintstone . . .

BARBIE BEE BLAIR
BINARY BIG BROTHER

It takes approximately two million flowers for a bee to make one pound of honey. And it takes 12 bees their entire lifetimes to make one teaspoonful. European settlers introduced European honey bees (*Apis mellifera*) to the USA (New England) in 1638 where Native Americans called them 'white man's flies'. A honey bee's wings beat at 11,400 times per minute – 190 times per second – which is what makes the buzzing noise. If we could walk at the same pace – 190 paces per second (the average human walking pace is 30 inches) – we would travel at nearly 324 mph. That means we'd be able to walk right around the equator of the Earth in just under four days.

In another scaling-up example, the world-famous Barbie doll can be shown to be worryingly disproportionate. If she were made life-sized (using her head as a gauge) her vital statistics would be 39–23–33 and she would be 7 feet 2 inches tall.

In the mid-1940s husband and wife Ruth and Elliot Handler owned a company that made wooden picture frames. Elliot began to use the scraps of leftover wood to make doll furniture and in 1945 joined with a close friend, Harold Mattson, to form a toy-making company. The company name was Mattel (Matt for Mattson and el for Elliot).

Then, in the mid-1950s, Ruth Handler came across a German doll called Lilli while visiting Europe. She was based on a cartoon character created by Reinhard Beuthien for the newspaper *Bild* and was quite unlike other dolls – which tended to be babies or young children – in that she was an adult and came with an extensive wardrobe. This inspired Ruth to have Mattel design a doll to her specifications. She then hired fashion designer Charlotte Johnson to create a wardrobe. A patent was obtained in 1958 and the doll was launched at the 1959 New York Toy Show. The doll was named Barbie after the Handlers' daughter. A few years later Barbie's boyfriend appeared. In a strangely incestuous move, he was named after Ruth and Elliot's son Ken.

Barbie has sold millions of units over the years but her popularity seems to be waning against other dolls such as Bratz and computer games. Ruth Handler's fortunes have also suffered: in 1978 she was found guilty of conspiracy, mail fraud and falsifying statements for which she received a 41-year suspended sentence, a $57,000 suspended fine and 2500 hours of community service. She left Mattel and the toy industry behind and started manufacturing artificial breasts for cancer victims instead.

In 2001 Barbie appeared in her first feature film, *Barbie in the Nutcracker*. But the curse of Hollywood struck in 2004, when it was announced that she and Ken had split after 43 years together. The couple's 'business manager', Russell Arons, vice president of marketing at Mattel, said that Barbie and Ken felt that it was 'time to spend some quality time apart'. Of course, it was a publicity stunt in an attempt to drum up sales.

Over the years Barbie has adopted many different personas with special-edition figures dressed as various goddesses, Madame de Pompadour, Marilyn Monroe, Cruella de Vil and various other Disney characters, the *X Files'* Mulder and Scully, Dorothy from *The Wizard of Oz* and as a leather-clad biker chick for the best-selling Harley-Davidson Barbie. However, despite all her various guises, she has always remained Barbie Millicent Roberts from Willows, Wisconsin, which is the home town of Ruth and Elliot Handler. Coincidentally (or maybe not) Wisconsin was also the birthplace of Harley-Davidson motorcycles.

The first production Harley-Davidson motorcycle was created in 1903 by William S. Harley and brothers Arthur and Walter Davidson, and an American icon was born. To begin with, it was praised simply as a record-breaking performance machine: in 1908 a Harley set an economy record of 188.234 miles per gallon. It also took first place in seven major motorcycle races in 1910 and a Harley-Davidson Sidecar won both the Pike's Peak race in 1916 and the 1922 Adelaide to Melbourne South Australia race. The 1920s saw the first appearance of the teardrop- or 'fat slug'-shaped fuel tank, and the eagle wing logo appeared just a few years later. The bike's popularity was also aided by films such as *Easy Rider* (1969), which helped cement the motorcycle's image as a metaphor for freedom and the counterculture revolution.

Which makes you wonder why ex-British prime minister Tony Blair had a Harley-Davidson-shaped telephone (a present from deputy John Prescott) on his desk during his tenure at Downing Street. A secret yearning to throw off the shackles of state and ride off into the sunset maybe?

Another Blair, Eric Arthur Blair, was born in 1903, the same year as the Harley-Davidson. He later took on the pen name of George Orwell and was the author of *Nineteen Eighty-Four*, a story about one man's fight against a totalitarian state and the ultimate counter-culture book.[15] The book has been made into several films, radio and TV series and a concept album by Rick Wakeman. As a result the terms Big Brother and Room 101 have entered popular culture and have also been used as the names of TV shows.

Room 101 is produced by the BBC, which means that it has 'come home' in a way. Orwell worked at the BBC between 1941 and 1943 writing propaganda and named his *Nineteen Eighty-Four* fictional torture chamber after Room 101 in BBC Broadcasting House (sadly the room no longer exists), where he had to sit

---

15 Has Orwell's nightmare vision of a society where cameras and computers spy on every person's movements come true? According to recent studies, Britain now has 4.2 million CCTV cameras – one for every fourteen people in the country – and 20 per cent of all security cameras globally. It has been calculated that we are all caught on camera an average of 300 times a day. And the flat where Orwell wrote *Nineteen Eighty-Four* is now within 200 yards of thirty-two CCTV cameras. Eek.

through many interminable meetings. In a curious twist, the 2005 UK version of the reality TV show *Big Brother* had a Room 101, where housemates had to perform tedious or odious tasks.

Incidentally, Erich Mielke, the last chairman of the Stasi (*Ministerium für Staatssicherheit* or Ministry for State Security of the former German Democratic Republic), was such a huge fan of Orwell's writing that he chose Room 101 of the Stasi building in East Berlin as his office. The building is now the Stasi museum, although it was trashed by jubilant Germans after the fall of the Berlin Wall.

The Stasi was widely feared and one of the most effective secret police and intelligence agencies of all time. At its peak it employed 91,000 people and 300,000 informants and kept records on some six million people (including an archive of fingerprints, sweat and body odour samples), around a third of East Germany's population. About one in 50 East Germans collaborated with the Stasi . . . as if they had a choice. The Stasi used torture and intimidation to stifle dissent. It has even been claimed that it intentionally exposed political dissidents to radiation so that they could track their movements using Geiger counters and because the radiation would eventually cause fatal cancers.

The Stasi successfully planted spies in every level of the West German government, one such being Günter Guillaume, who rose so high that he became a close aide to Chancellor Willy Brandt. When Guillaume was exposed in 1974, Brandt was forced to resign. Guillaume was sent back to East Germany in 1981 in return for the release of West German spies. He was welcomed home as a hero and trained future spies.

One of the earliest British spies is alleged to have been playwright and poet Christopher Marlowe (1564–93). Marlowe, known to his friends as Kit, was born in Canterbury, Kent and educated at the Kings School and later at Corpus Christi College, Cambridge. The university at first refused to award him his master's degree as they claimed that he had secretly become a Catholic having studied at a Catholic college in Rheims, France (unlikely, as evidence indicates that Marlowe was both gay and atheist). But then a curious thing happened ... The Privy Council, the Queen's advisers, stepped in and ordered the university to reconsider because of Marlowe's 'faithful dealing and good service' to the Queen. This led to the belief that Marlowe had been in France working for Elizabeth I as a spy and secret agent – possibly as part of Sir Francis Walsingham's intelligence service.

In 1592 Marlowe was arrested in the Netherlands for allegedly attempting to counterfeit coins but was released without charge. Then, the following year, he was accused of penning a series of libellous and heretical letters and was arrested at the home of Thomas Walsingham, the cousin of the head of state espionage. He was again released but only if he attended the Privy Council daily, an early form of signing in at a police station. Shortly after this, Marlowe was murdered.

Marlowe's death was as mysterious as his life. One version says he was stabbed during a drunken bar brawl (often still cited as the official story). Another, that he was killed by a gay lover. More intriguing, however, is evidence from the coroner's report at the time, which states that Marlowe had spent the day he died at a house owned by the Walsinghams and had been meeting three of Walsingham's men.

We will probably never know the whole truth about Marlowe's life and death. The conflicting reports have suggested to some researchers and historians that he may even have faked his own death and adopted a new identity – a kind of Elizabethan witness protection programme – to escape from enemies he'd made. One popular theory is that the new identity was one William Shakespeare.

There are convincing reasons to doubt the authenticity of Shakespeare's plays. Firstly, there is almost no evidence that Shakespeare even existed. No letters, diaries or other documents exist that were written by him; there are large gaps in his personal history; there is no record of his admission at any school, college or university; and his otherwise comprehensive last will and testament failed to mention his shares in the Globe and Blackfriars Theatres. He is supposed to have been a commoner, yet he apparently had a vocabulary of approximately 29,000 different words, almost six times as large as that used for the King James Bible. This has led to claims that Shakespeare was either a pseudonym for another writer or that the actual William Shakespeare was a frontman for someone who wished to remain anonymous. Kit Marlowe is a likely candidate as, before Shakespeare, he was one of the foremost writers of his day. Other candidates include William Stanley (6th Earl of Derby), Edward de Vere (17th Earl of Oxford), Queen Elizabeth I herself and Francis Bacon.

Francis Bacon, 1st Viscount St Albans (1561–1626), was a true Renaissance man. He was a writer, a statesman, a philosopher and a scientist (there are also theories that he was the illegitimate son of Elizabeth I and Robert Dudley, Earl of Leicester). He was a pioneer of the scientific method, using correctly staged experiments and recording the results against proper controls and measures. As the result, he and his peers began the process of separating true science from magic, alchemy and other long-held traditional beliefs. He even died as the result of an experiment. He caught pneumonia after spending a protracted time stuffing a bird with snow to see whether cold temperatures could be used to preserve meat. Yes, Francis Bacon is the father of refrigeration.

He is also in one way the father of computers as he came up with the earliest version of binary numbers. Although the Chinese had designed something akin to binary for producing the hexagrams used in the *I Ching*, it was Bacon who first proposed the idea of a binary system that could be used for encoding anything 'provided those objects be capable of a twofold difference only'.[16] The binary system we know today –

---

16 *The Advancement of Learning* (1605).

using 0 and 1 – was developed a few years later by Gottfried Leibniz.

The number 101 is five expressed in binary and coincidentally it took five years, between 1937 and 1942, to build the first electronic digital computer. It was constructed by John Vincent Atanasoff and Clifford Berry at Iowa State University and incorporated several major innovations in computing, such as the use of binary arithmetic. The term 'bit' used in computing is short for binary digit. This pioneering machine was called the Atanasoff-Berry Computer or ABC.

ABC was the name of a band that had a string of hits throughout the early to mid-1980s . . . around the time Winston Smith would have been languishing in Room 101. The band happily straddled punk and the so-called New Romantics while still nodding a head to the soul greats of the past. They were led by flamboyant gold lamé-suited frontman Martin Fry. Around 1985 the band was forced to take a break while Fry was treated for Hodgkin's lymphoma, formerly known as Hodgkin's disease. Hodgkin's was one of the first cancers to become curable by a combination of chemotherapy and a cocktail of different drugs to battle different aspects of the cancer's behaviour. One of these drugs is Vincristine, an alkaloid obtained from the sap of a plant called the Madagascar periwinkle. The periwinkle is easy to grow and in some places has become invasive. This is partly due to the fact that it is self-propagating. In other words, it does not require birds, wind or insects to disperse its seeds or for pollination.

The process of pollination by insects is called entomophily. Entomophilous plants produce pollen that is larger than that of plants that use the wind. It's also of more nutritional value to insects – a strong insect will carry the pollen further. Many insects, such as bees, eat both pollen and nectar. Bees also collect pollen in 'baskets' – special sticky hairs on their legs – so that it can be taken back to the hive to feed the young. In order to make themselves more appealing to insects many flowers carry strong scents. Colour is used to attract too. Insects can see in the ultraviolet part of the electromagnetic spectrum so many plants have distinct and striking patterns on their flowers invisible to us (except under UV light) but attractive to the insects.

Nectar is a sugar-rich liquid produced in glands called nectaries. These are generally at the base of the flower so that pollen-dusted nectar eaters are made to brush against the flower's reproductive structures (anthers and pistil). Nectar is the sugar source used by bees when making honey.

It takes approximately two million flowers for a bee . . .

TICK TOCK
CHOPSTICKS CLOCKS

In 1877, when she was just 16, Euphemia Allen wrote a little tune that became known the world over to budding pianists. The tune was a simple waltz called 'Chopsticks'.

Chopsticks, as eating utensils, are believed to have been developed and used as long as 5000 years ago. Chinese tradition holds that mealtimes are events to promote social harmony through the gathering of family and friends. Blades are associated with violence and conflict; it is therefore considered inappropriate for any implement designed to cut, such as a knife, or stab (the fork resembles several traditional weapons such as tridents and *sai* daggers) to be used at the dining table. Chopsticks never have pointed ends for the same reason.

The Standard Chinese word for chopsticks is *kuàizi* or *kuài'er*, which literally means 'bamboo-objects for eating quickly'. In China alone an estimated 45 billion pairs of disposable chopsticks are used and thrown away annually. This adds up to 2.2 million cubic yards of timber or 25 million fully grown trees every year. To encourage people to reuse their chopsticks a 5 per cent tax was added to the price in April 2006.

Not quite as many trees, but still a substantial 300,000, are cut down yearly across the USA just to produce all of the paper needed for tax forms (and the instructions on how to complete them). To meet the needs of paper consumers and to clear land for cattle to graze on (for beef production), millions upon millions of trees are felled every year. The charity Oxfam states that an estimated 67 acres of forest are lost every minute – that's an area equivalent to 37 football pitches.

Oxfam began life in 1942 as the Oxford Committee for Famine Relief, formed alongside a number of other British organizations to highlight the problems created by the Nazi occupation of various countries. It set out to raise awareness and money, becoming a registered charity in 1943. Its first appeal, Greek Week, raised £12,700 for the Greek Red Cross. Among the many celebrities who support Oxfam as ambassadors are the members of UK band Coldplay.

The lead singer of Coldplay is Chris Martin. His great-great-grandfather was William Willett, the man who convinced Parliament to introduce British Summer Time (BST). Willett was a London builder from Petts Wood in Kent. In 1907 he circulated a pamphlet to Members of Parliament, town councils, businesses and other organizations in which he stated that the nation's health and happiness could be improved by longer exposure to the Sun. To do this, he proposed Daylight Saving Time, whereby the clocks would be moved forward twenty minutes on each of four Sundays in April. Then, the same would happen, but in reverse, on Sundays in September. The idea was initially ridiculed but the onset of World War I brought the idea out of limbo.

In May 1916 Daylight Saving Time was introduced as a way of saving money on lighting. Within a week almost every other country was doing it too. But sadly William never saw his idea put into effect as he died in 1915. These days, his idea has become British Summer Time (although the older original name is still used in the USA), with the clocks turned forward an hour on the last Sunday in March, and brought back an hour to Greenwich Mean Time (GMT) on the last Sunday in October.

'Clocks' was one of Coldplay's biggest hits.

The father of the modern mechanical clock was the Dutch scientist Christian Huygens, who in 1656 made the first pendulum clock. In 1657 he developed the balance wheel and spring assembly, which is still found in some of today's clocks and watches. Huygens' first clock had an error rate of less than one minute a day. Later refinements reduced this margin of error to less than ten seconds a day.

The technical name for an instrument that measures time is a chronograph or chronometer, but they have slightly different functions. A chronograph is a timepiece with both timekeeping and stopwatch functions. A chronometer is a timepiece accurate enough to be used in navigation. The prefix chron- is used at the front of many words relating to time like chronology, chronic and chronicle, and appears in words like anachronism. It comes from Chronos, or Kronos, the god of time in classical Greek mythology. A prophecy stated that he would be overthrown by his own son, so Chronos ate all of his children as soon as they were born. But his wife, Rhea, swapped the youngest, Zeus, for a rock wrapped in a blanket. (Poseidon, as you

know, substituted a small horse and escaped too.)
When Zeus grew up, he confronted his estranged (and
surprised) father and forced him to vomit up all of his
brothers and sisters. He then led a war against
Chronos' people – the Titans – and imprisoned them.
Later, Zeus relented and made Chronos the king of
the Elysian Islands, home of the blessed dead.

The story is immortalized in the French opera
Jupiter, Vainqueur des Titans,[17] written in 1745 by
François Colin de Blamont and Bernard de Bury. It
was written in the unique style of the French *tragédie
lyrique* (occasionally also known as *tragédie en
musique*). This style was created by Jean-Baptiste
Lully, a composer who spent most of his life working
in the court of Louis XIV and who founded the French
National Opera. Lully died at the age of 55 following
a silly accident during which he hit his foot with the
staff that he was using to beat out time (the use of a
staff was common practice before the invention of the
conductor's baton). He developed an abscess on a toe
that turned gangrenous but refused to have the infected
toe amputated. The infection spread and he died in
1687.

---

17 Jupiter was the Roman name for Zeus, king of the gods.

Lully took French citizenship in 1661, along with a French name. However, he was actually Italian by birth (1632) and was christened Giovanni Battista Lulli. He is commemorated in the pseudonym Arthur de Lulli, which was used by British composer Euphemia Allen (1861–1949).

In 1877, when she was just 16, Euphemia Allen wrote a little tune . . .

BEAM ME UP, SHERLOCK

UFO stands for unidentified flying object. It's a more generally accepted term these days than flying saucer. The term flying saucer is generally (and wrongly) attributed to Kenneth A. Arnold, a private pilot from Boise, Idaho, whose famous sighting is often credited in the media as the 'first UFO sighting'. This is also wrong as there were many less-publicized sightings before it.

On 24 June 1947 Arnold was flying his plane near Mount Rainier, Washington when he reported seeing nine odd-looking objects flying in a chain. They were very bright and travelling very, very fast. He described their erratic flight patterns as 'like a saucer if you skip it across the water' but he was misquoted in the press and the flying saucer was born. In fact, the 'craft' that

Arnold claimed to have seen were a crescent-Moon shape with a point midway along the concave curve, so that each looked a little like a stylized number three.

UFO aficionados, or ufologists, fall into two general camps – those who believe that UFOs are alien space-craft, and those who think they are secret man-made vehicles, possibly utilizing alternative fuel sources, being tested by the military or government. And many people have noted the similarity of Arnold's sighting to the (then) experimental 'flying wing' design of aircraft such as the German Horten HO229 and the US Nor-throp YB-49. Flying wing experiments ultimately led to the development of the Lockheed Spirit 'stealth' bomber now in active service. Its designation is B2.

Vitamin B2, also known as riboflavin or vitamin G, is essential for good health. It helps the body to metabolize fats, proteins and carbohydrates and also aids production of red blood cells. As an additive, its E-number is E101.

E-numbers are codes for food additives used throughout the European Union (hence the E). E100–E199 are food colours, E200–E299 are preservatives, E300–E399 are antioxidants and acidity regulators, E400–E499 are thickeners, stabilizers and emulsifiers, E500–E599 are acidity regulators and anti-caking agents, E600–E699 are flavour enhancers and E900–E1999 are the worryingly named 'miscellaneous and additional chemicals'. In the USA the Food and Drug Administration (FDA) issues equivalent codes beginning with the prefix FD&C, from the Federal Food, Drug and Cosmetic Act of 1938. For example, tartrazine is E102 in the UK, but in the USA is generally referred to as FD&C Yellow No. 5.

The Codex Alimentarius Commission is developing the International Numbering System (INS) for food additives. This will largely use the same numbers as the current European system but will drop the E prefix.

Codex alimentarius is Latin for food law or food code. The alimentary canal is the name given to the 'food canal', the 25 feet of gut inside each human being. Food starts its journey at the mouth and passes through the pharynx, oesophagus, stomach, small intestine (duodenum, jejunum and ileum), large intestine (caecum, colon and sigmoid flexure) before arriving finally at the rectum and anus.

The similarity between the words alimentary and elementary makes it a commonly misspelled word (along with access/excess, effect/affect and others). The similarity has often been used for puns. For example, in the James Bond movie *Diamonds Are*

Forever some of the gemstones in question are hidden inside a corpse. When Felix Leiter asks Bond where the diamonds are, he replies, 'Alimentary, my dear Leiter,' a spoof on the famous catchphrase of fictional detective Sherlock Holmes.[18]

Incidentally, although similar in pronunciation, the two words are entirely unrelated. One comes from the Latin *alimentum* meaning food; the other from *elementum*, meaning part of a series or component. Elementary is taken to mean the basic or lowest or simplest form of something. Because all matter can be broken down into atoms, these are known as elementary particles. The substances made of atoms are known as elements. Interestingly, any skill broken down to its most basic level in order to teach it gets the designation 101 in US colleges – for example, Engineering 101, History 101. The reason why seems to be lost in time but one theory states that it's shorthand for year one, day one or level one, lesson one. E101 is also the designation of vitamin B2, you may recall.

---

18 The film's producer, Cubby Broccoli, was unsure whether to include this pun in the final cut. He was reassured by the writers that it was worth it, but at the premiere at the Grauman Chinese Theatre in Los Angeles only two people at the front laughed. The writers claimed success. 'Big deal,' said Broccoli. 'Two doctors!'

Although 'Elementary, my dear Watson' may be the most quoted of Sherlock Holmes' various catchphrases, he never uttered those words in any of Sir Arthur Conan Doyle's novels and short stories. Not once. And just as Sherlock Holmes never said 'Elementary, my dear Watson' and Kenneth Arnold never said 'flying saucers', Captain Kirk never said 'Beam me up, Scotty' in any episode of *Star Trek* ever. But a version of Holmes' erroneous catchphrase did make it as a *Star Trek* episode title.

In the episode 'Elementary Dear Data' (1988) the *Next Generation* crew plays out a Sherlock Holmes mystery on the holodeck. Then, in a later episode, 'Ship in a Bottle' (1993), a holographic Professor Moriarty seizes control of the USS *Enterprise*. Oh, and in the 1967 original *Star Trek* episode 'Tomorrow Is Yesterday' the *Enterprise* travels back in time to Earth in 1969 and is spotted as . . . a UFO.

Star Trek was one of three major sci-fi series that began in the 1960s. *Trek* began in 1966. *Dr Who* began in 1963. And *Thunderbirds* began in 1965.

Thunderbirds was Gerry Anderson's best-loved and most successful TV series. Amazingly, it ran for only 32 episodes and spawned two feature films (three if you count the 2003 movie directed by Jonathan Frakes

– Commander Riker in *Star Trek – The Next Generation*). The series featured the adventures of a secret organization called International Rescue. The brainchild of retired astronaut and entrepreneur Jeff Tracy and based on a privately owned island somewhere in the South Seas, International Rescue sent out its extraordinary super-advanced rescue machines – the Thunderbirds of the title – to tackle any disaster from collapsing oil rigs to damaged spacecraft hurtling toward the Sun. Jeff's five sons operated the Thunderbirds, occasionally assisted by their designer, Homer Newton III, known as Brains, and the bizarrely named Tin-Tin Kyrano, daughter of the Tracy family house-manager-cum-chef.

The Tracy boys were all named after real US astronauts from the *Mercury* missions: John Glenn Tracy, Scott Carpenter Tracy, Virgil Grissom Tracy, Alan Shepard Tracy and Gordon Cooper Tracy. Jeff Tracy lost his wife shortly after Alan's birth. Her name was Lucille.

Thunderbirds was filmed using advanced marionettes operated by some of the best puppeteers in the world. Gerry Anderson called this format for making TV programmes 'supermarionation' and used it on *The Adventures of Twizzle*, *Torchy the Battery Boy*, *Four*

Feather Falls, Supercar, Fireball XL5, Stingray, Captain Scarlet, Joe 90 and *The Secret Service* before moving away from puppets to live actors in the 1970s. His first live action series was set in the year 1980 and told the story of another secret group – SHADO (Supreme Headquarters Alien Defence Organization) – and its fight to save us all from green-skinned alien invaders bent upon harvesting our internal organs for spare-part surgery. The series was called *UFO*.

UFO stands for unidentified flying object . . .

RED, RED WINE AND RED, RED INDIANS

The avocado (*Persea americana*) or alligator pear takes its name from the Nahuatl (the language used by the Aztecs) word *ahuacatl*, meaning testicle, which is believed to be due to its scrotal shape. The related word *ahuacamolli* means avocado soup or avocado sauce and is the origin of the word guacamole. So, technically, guacamole translates as 'testicle sauce'.

Amazingly, for such a popular food, avocado is actually poisonous. In humans the effects are negligible (unless there is an allergic reaction) but animals can be severely harmed or even die if they eat it. The toxic substance is an oil called persin which is found in the stone and leaches out into the fruit. In birds it produces lethargy, breathing difficulties and sudden death. In rabbits, goats, cattle and horses it can cause inflammation of the mammary glands and a build-up of fluid around the heart. Many other plants, and plant derivatives, that humans enjoy are also poisonous to animals including chocolate, onions, macadamia nuts, grapes and raisins. Dogs are particularly affected by chocolate and Christmas time sees many fatalities as family pets are fed by children or steal ornaments from the tree. In 2006 UK vets answered 790 emergency calls about chocolate poisoning.

In their excellently named book *The Ghosts of Evolution: Nonsensical Fruit, Missing Partners and Other Ecological Anachronisms* (2002) Connie Barlow and Paul Martin suggest that the avocado co-evolved with large mammals, now extinct, that swallowed the fruit whole and excreted the seed in dung, ready to sprout. The animals in question would have been South American herbivorous gomphotheres – several species of large elephant-like creatures – and giant ground sloths.

Ground sloths are extinct relatives of the modern tree sloths and three-toed sloths. They were larger than modern elephants, weighing more than five tons and able to stand as high as 17 feet. They were equipped with dangerously long sharp claws. They first appeared about 35 million years ago in what is now southern Argentina but there is some evidence to show that they may have died out as recently as 1550 in Hispaniola and Cuba ... which means that they were still around when Christopher Columbus arrived.

Columbus (1451–1506) first arrived in the Americas in 1492 but did not actually set foot upon the American mainland until 1498 during his third voyage. His first voyage took him only to the aforementioned Hispaniola and Cuba and one of the islands in the Bahamas, though no one is sure which. Columbus was not the first European explorer to reach America but he did open up the trade routes that created modern America. Among the many who reached the continent before him was the Viking explorer Leif Ericson some four centuries before, who established a settlement called Vinland in what is now L'Anse aux Meadows, Newfoundland, Canada.

Ericson, or Erickson, or Ericsson, or Eriksson was born in Iceland around 970, a son of Erik the Red. He had two younger brothers called Thorvaldr and Thorsteinn, and one sister, Freydís. He married a woman named Thorgunna, and they had a son, Thorkell Leifsson.

Iceland has a fascinating naming convention. Surnames are formed by taking the father's forename and suffixing it with *son* if a boy or *dóttir* if a girl. Hence, Björk Guðmundsdóttir is Bjork, daughter of Guð-mund. And the late Magnus Magnusson was Magnus, son of Magnus. It means that family members can all have different surnames. Let's create an imaginary family to demonstrate. Dad is Peter. His father was called Thomas. So Dad is Peter Thomasson. His wife, Debbie, has a father called John. So Mum is Debbie Johnsdóttir. Their children are Melanie Petersdóttir and Andrew Petersson. Occasionally, a child will take their name from mother rather than father; for instance, a single mother who wants to distance herself from the father. Some feminists have also chosen to take their mother's name as a political stand. But the convention is still the same, so Janet, daughter of Mary, would be Janet Marysdóttir. This system means that Icelandic people usually greet each other by forename rather than surname, even in a formal setting. Magnus Mag-nusson would be greeted as Magnus or Mr Magnus, for instance. And Bjork is not a stage name like Bono; it's actually how she would normally be addressed. All of this means that the Icelandic telephone book is unique in listing people by their forenames, rather than surnames. And it's why Leif Ericson's son was called Thorkell Leifsson.

Leif Erickson was the stage name of American actor William Anderson (1911–86), best known for playing patriarch Big John Cannon in the Western TV series *The High Chaparral*, which ran 1967–71. In the series the part of Cochise was played by Nino Cochise, the grandson of the Cochise who fought in the Apache wars. Born in 1874, Nino was 92 years old at the time of being cast, was missing one leg, and needed to be helped into and out of the saddle . . . but he got the role anyway.

Nowadays, we would refer to Cochise as a Native American, but at the time *High Chaparral* was set, the common term was Indian or Red Indian. This comes from the fact that when Columbus arrived in the so-called New World, he believed that he had reached India, the original destination of his voyage.

The name Cochise is Apache for hardwood. The term hardwood means wood from broad-leaved (mostly deciduous) trees. Softwood generally comes from evergreen, or coniferous, trees. Lignum vitae is considered the hardest commercial hardwood. It is not only extremely hard, but also very heavy and will sink in water. Due to its weight, lignum vitae (also known as ironwood) was used to make the ribs of Ernest Shackleton's Antarctic exploring ship *Endurance*, and for old-fashioned police truncheons and staves. It also has some medicinal properties and in T. H. White's version of the Artus/Arthurian saga *The Once and Future King* lignum vitae is reported to have magical powers and Merlin the magician's staff was made from it. In the world of cricket lignum vitae is used to make so-called heavy bails, used in matches during windy conditions.

Cricket bails consist of a fatter middle section called the barrel and narrow protrusions at each end called spigots. The terms come from the wine industry. Wine is aged in wooden barrels made of hardwood, usually oak. Olivier Merlin is widely regarded as being one of the very finest winemakers in the Mâconnais, in the southern part of the Burgundy region in France. Burgundy is a shade of dark red associated with the wine of the same name, which in turn is named after the Burgundy region. The rich colour of the wine is created by pressing red Pinot Noir grapes.

Grapes are a form of berry. In botany, a berry is defined as a fruit in which the entire ovary wall ripens into an edible pericarp, the tougher outer layer surrounding a fleshy interior. The seeds are embedded in the flesh of the ovary. In other words, a berry is a single fruit with seeds inside, not a composite of lots of smaller fruits. All of which means that a lot of the things we call berries – like strawberries, blackberries and raspberries – aren't berries at all. True berries include grapes, blackcurrants, gooseberries, cranberries, lychees, guavas, aubergines, tomatoes, peppers and avocados.

The avocado (*Persea americana*) or alligator pear takes its name . . .

Round 12

PEACHY! AND I MEAN THAT MOST SINCERELY, FOLKS . . .

James and the Giant Peach is a children's book written by Roald Dahl originally published in 1961. The content – particularly the mental and physical abuse of the child hero James Henry Trotter – means that it has always provoked controversy. In this, it is not alone. Many of Dahl's books have been the target of censors and several appear on the American Library Association list, the '100 Most Frequently Challenged Books of 1990–2000'. Other 'frequently challenged books' on the list include the Harry Potter books (number 7), *Heather Has Two Mommies* by Leslea Newman (11), *Where's Waldo?* by Martin Hanford (88) and, because of alleged racism (even though the book is fundamentally anti-slavery) *The Adventures of Huc-*

kleberry Finn by Mark Twain (5). Dahl's *The Witches* comes in at number 27 (one higher than *The New Joy of Gay Sex* by Charles Silverstein at 28) and *James and the Giant Peach* at number 56.

Peaches Honeyblossom Geldof is the second daughter of Sir Bob Geldof and his late ex-wife Paula Yates. She is one of four sisters all with famously bizarre names, the others being Fifi Trixibelle, Little Pixie and Heavenly Hiraani Tiger Lily. Tiger Lily, as she prefers to be known, is a half-sister, her father being the late Michael Hutchence of Australian rock band INXS. Hutchence died in bizarre circumstances in 1997, officially as the result of a suicide.

Paula Yates (who had split from Geldof) didn't accept the suicide verdict for Hutchence and never truly recovered from his death, suffering frequent bouts of depression. She was dealt a further blow when she discovered, by way of a paternity test, that her own natural father was not religious TV broadcaster Jess Yates, but television quiz show host Hughie Green. Shortly after this announcement in 2000 she was found dead. The coroner recorded a verdict of accidental heroin overdose.

Hughie Green is most famous for hosting the long-running new talent show *Opportunity Knocks*, which ran in various forms on several different TV channels between 1957 and 1990. The show discovered many new stars including singers Mary Hopkin, Bonnie Langford, Lena Zavaroni, Peters and Lee, poet Pam Ayres and comedian Freddie Starr.

A horse owned by Freddie Starr – Miinnehoma – won the Grand National Steeplechase in 1994, ridden by top jockey Richard Dunwoody. However, the most successful Grand National winner ever was Red Rum, the only horse in history to win the race three times. Red Rum also ran two other Grand Nationals, coming second in each. He lived to be 30 years old, died in 1995 and was buried next to the winning post at Aintree racetrack.

The name Red Rum is a reversal of the word murder and this has led some people to believe that the name was taken from the Stephen King book (and subsequent film by Stanley Kubrick) *The Shining*, in which a possessed child, Danny, repeats the word over and over again before writing it in lipstick on a bathroom door. However, King's book was written in 1977 while the racehorse was born (and named) in 1965.

This was a year when murder was very much on the minds of the American people as it was when the

USA's first real serial killer was caught. The Boston Strangler, as he came to be known, murdered 13 women between June 1962 and January 1964. What made the Strangler's crimes more terrifying than the killings of someone like Jack the Ripper was that anyone was a potential target: the victims were not prostitutes or vagrants, but respectable, middle-aged or elderly women attacked in their own homes.

Albert DeSalvo must have seemed the perfect suspect when he confessed in March 1965. He had already been arrested and charged in November 1964 for a series of rapes in Connecticut known as the 'green man' offences because the attacker wore green overalls. However, there was no evidence to substantiate his confession to the stranglings, and he stood trial only for the green man and other unrelated robbery offences. He was sent to prison for life in 1967, but was murdered in his cell six years later, being stabbed through the heart. His killer has never been identified.

Casey Sherman, a nephew of the Strangler's final victim, Mary Sullivan, has spent years investigating the case. He is convinced that DeSalvo was a scapegoat used by certain senior police officers to clear up the case and advance their own careers. He believes that DeSalvo was about to tell the real story when he was murdered. Sherman also states that his investigations have led him to a possible suspect, a man who was the police's prime candidate in 1964, prior to DeSalvo's arrest, and who is now living in northern New England . . .

The Guildford Stranglers was the original name of British punk band The Stranglers, who formed in Surrey in 1974. The original line-up of Hugh Cornwell, Jean-Jacques Burnel, Dave Greenfield and Jet Black (aka Brian Duffy) had a string of hits including 'Strange Little Girl', 'Golden Brown', 'Something Better Change', 'No More Heroes' and 'Peaches'. The latter song features the slang use of peach to describe an attractive woman. The term is also used to describe the female buttocks due to a similarity with the fruit (*Prunus persica*), which has a distinctive bottom-like cleft.

Peaches originated in China and have been cultivated for at least 3000 years. The native, wild peach is small, fuzzy-skinned and quite sour. The peach tree was seen as the tree of life and the peach itself is a symbol of immortality in Chinese culture. To this day new brides carry peach blossom during the marriage ceremony. Peaches made their way out into the rest of the world via the silk roads to Persia (now Iran), hence the scientific name *Prunus persica*. Peach varieties are broadly classed as either clingstones or freestones depending on how hard it is to pull the stone away from the flesh. The nectarine is a variant form with a smooth skin. World production totals about 5.4 million tons annually, with China, the United States and Italy being the leading producers.

James and the Giant Peach is a children's book written by Roald Dahl . . .

UNLUCKY FOR SOME . . . UNTRUE FOR OTHERS

During production of the 1939 film *The Wizard of Oz*, a coat purchased from a second-hand store for the costume of Professor Marvel was later discovered to have once belonged to L. Frank Baum, the author of the original children's book upon which the film is based. But this may be an urban myth.[19]

Baum's first name was Lyman (that bit is true).

When Baum was writing for the *Aberdeen Saturday Pioneer* newspaper, he once described a woman as having a 'roughish smile' when he meant to write 'roguish smile'. As he was describing a bride at her wedding, the husband challenged Baum to a duel. The two men stood back to back, ready to walk ten paces,

---

19 Thanks to the urban myths website www.snopes.com for much of the information in this Round.

turn and shoot. Baum panicked and his walk turned into a run, but then a man stopped him and said, 'You fool! The other guy's running too!'

But this may also be an urban myth.

Talking of duels, there is a story that the script of the film *Raiders of the Lost Ark* originally called for an extended duel between Indiana Jones and an Arab swordsman. However, because actor Harrison Ford was suffering from dysentery, director Steven Spielberg suggested that Indy simply pulled out his gun and shot the swordsman. This impromptu rewrite provided one of the film's best comic moments.

Surprisingly, this particular story is entirely true.

And, talking of dysentery ... in 2000 an email originating from Schwab Corporate Headquarters warned the public about an unidentified person posting dangerous objects randomly to the public. The packages – which were blue and marked with the words The Klingerman Foundation – contained a free sponge. But the sponge was infected with the deadly Klingerman virus. The virus caused severe dysentery and, ultimately, death.

This was an urban myth and the virus does not exist.

The name Klingerman is German in origin and first

appeared in Swabia – Schwaben or Schwabenland in German, which sounds oddly like Schwab, the name of the corporation supposedly behind the virus. 'Schwab' means ravine or gorge.

To gorge, when used as a verb, means to eat heavily, and that's something that tapeworms do well. So much so that a person infected with tapeworms can eat like a horse but still die of malnutrition as the worms get the lion's share. Or, in this case, the worms' share. The symptoms of tapeworm infestation so resemble some viral infections that it is sometimes mistaken for a disease.

A few years ago a company put out sure-fire diet pills, guaranteed to help you to lose weight in no time. People began to take these pills and, sure enough, were losing weight in no time. But after a few weeks some people began to lose too much weight. The government investigated and when they opened the pills found tapeworm eggs. The story gets worse . . . Tapeworms are notoriously difficult to get rid of. The most effective method is to starve the infected person for days, then set a bowl of hot milk in front of them. After a while the tapeworm begins to come up the throat because it can smell the milk. By the patient keeping his mouth open, and by moving the bowl further and further away, the tapeworm eventually is expelled.

Surely this must be an urban myth?

Of course it is. Well ... almost. The milk story is utter nonsense of course, but there is a nugget of truth at the heart of the diet story. As unlikely as this may sound, there is some evidence that tapeworm diet pills were marketed in the United States between 1900 and 1920. Eek.

Tapeworms are an extreme example of the lengths people will go to in order to lose weight. Fads and fashions come and go, and one of the most popular of recent years was the Atkins Diet. Champion of the carb-free diet, Dr Robert Atkins' methods were attacked many times during his lifetime by other dietary experts who claimed that his high-protein and fat-rich diet scheme would lead to heart attacks as well as weight loss. With a large dollop of irony, Atkins died of a heart attack. Allegedly.

The official story is that Atkins died on 17 April 2003 at the age of 72 after sustaining head injuries in a fall outside his New York clinic. However, revelations in February 2004 from the city medical examiner's report let slip the information that Atkins had suffered a heart attack, congestive heart failure and hypertension before his death. However, an autopsy was not performed on him because of family objections to the procedure. Consequently, the medical examiner conducted only an external exam and a review of Atkins' hospital records.

So we'll have to chalk that one up as a maybe.

Autopsies are a great way of debunking urban myths. Among the more well-known are the story that singer Mama Cass died by choking on a ham sandwich (autopsy showed she died of heart failure); that Catharine the Great died while having sex with a horse (actually, a cerebral haemorrhage); and that John Wayne died from having 40 pounds of impacted faecal matter in his intestine (cancer, sorry). Wayne didn't have an autopsy as his aggressive terminal cancer was a matter of proven fact, but I had to mention it as the story is so patently absurd. There are real medical cases of people suffering extreme abdominal pain from just 1 pound of impacted faeces. So 40 pounds is ridiculous. Even more silly is the story that Elvis Presley was found to have 60 pounds of the same. It's just another urban myth.

Ridiculous stories about unfeasible amounts of impacted faecal matter are often used as 'proof' that man is not meant to be a carnivore (sorry, Dr Atkins) and as promotion for supposedly healthy therapies like colonic irrigation. This particular treatment is often cited as a preventative measure against colon cancer though there is no scientifically proven evidence of this. Nor is there any proof that drinking eight to ten glasses of water per day will prevent disease. The story is quite old but achieved some degree of credibility when advocated by a Dr Fereydoon Batmanghelidj, an Iranian physician whose personal creed is 'You are not ill – you are thirsty.' However, he has publicly admitted that he arrived at this theory by reading rather than research, and his claims seem more hopeful than scientific. Among the illnesses Batmanghelidj has listed as curable by drinking water are colon cancer, arthritis, migraines, hypertension, asthma and angina pectoris.

Angina pectoris is chest pain or discomfort that occurs when your heart muscle does not get enough blood. Angina commonly feels like pressure, or a squeezing pain, in your chest. The pain may also occur in your shoulders, arms, neck, jaw or back. It may also feel like indigestion. A severe bout can be the prelude to a heart attack.

Some 1.4 million people in England suffer from angina, 300,000 have heart attacks and more than

110,000 die as a result of heart problems every year. Among the many famous people who live or have lived with angina are Alfred Nobel, Bill Clinton, Richard Wagner and L. Frank Baum – author of *The Wizard of Oz*.

During production of the 1939 film *The Wizard of Oz* . . .

BACK IN ROOM 101

T he tallest building in the world (at time of writing) is called Taipei 101 and stands in Taipei City, Taiwan. From the ground to the structural top, the building is 1,671 feet high. It has five storeys underground and 101 storeys above ground, hence the name. However, it will not be the tallest for much longer . . . The Burj Dubai (Dubai Tower) currently under construction in the United Arab Emirates is already the tallest free-standing structure in the world (meaning any structure, building or otherwise, not supported by ropes, cables, etc.), having taken the 32-year record from the CN Tower in Toronto, Canada, and, when completed in late 2008, will easily be the tallest building on Earth. The exact final height of the Burj Dubai is being kept a secret as the builders do not want to provide competitors with a target to beat. However, figures released by a contractor on the project have suggested a height of around 2,684 feet, which would mean something like 160 storeys. If the building exceeds 2,297 feet, it will be the tallest land-based structure to have ever been built.

Previous holders of the world's tallest building title include the Petronas Towers in Kuala Lumpur, the Sears Tower in Chicago, the World Trade Center, the Empire State Building and the Eiffel Tower.

Alexandre Gustave Eiffel (1832–1923) designed many structures that have had great social, economic, and political impacts on the world. These include bridges, the great tower in Paris and the Statue of Liberty.

The Statue of Liberty is so well known and so iconic that it frequently makes appearances in movies. At the end of *Men in Black II* the statue's torch contains a giant 'neuralizer' which is used to wipe the memories of everyone in New York. In *The Day after Tomorrow* it can be seen buried in snow and ice. In 2008's *Cloverfield* its head is knocked off by the rampaging monster. There was even a film called *The Statue of Liberty*, which was nominated for an Oscar in 1985. Most famously, it appears in the climax of the 1968 movie version of *Planet of the Apes*, where it can be seen, ancient and wrecked, and protruding from a beach. Its appearance reveals to astronaut George Taylor (Charlton Heston) that he is not on another world but on Earth, albeit far in the future (AD 3978).

Taylor is one of four astronauts aboard the *Icarus* spacecraft, which crashes into a lake on a mysterious planet. The only female member of crew – Stewart – is found to be long dead. Taylor, Landon and Dodge, the three survivors, get to dry land, where they meet timid humans who cannot speak. A short while later they and the mute humans are hunted by talking apes on horseback. Taylor is captured; Dodge is killed and later mounted as a taxidermist's piece in a museum; Landon is given a lobotomy when it is discovered he can speak.

Hannibal Lecter, played by Anthony Hopkins, gives Ray Liotta a lobotomy and feeds him pieces of his own cooked brain in the film *Hannibal* (2001).

Colonel John 'Hannibal' Smith, played by George Peppard, was the leader of popular 1970s have-a-go heroes *The A-Team*. Peppard shot to fame in 1961 playing opposite Audrey Hepburn in the film *Breakfast at Tiffany's*.

Audrey Hepburn was born Audrey Kathleen Ruston in Brussels, Belgium. Her father was an Anglo-Irish banker called John Victor Hepburn-Ruston, her mother a Dutch aristocrat called Baroness Ella van Heemstra. Hepburn was a descendant of King Edward III of England.

Edward III was crowned on 1 February 1327 at the age of 14 and ruled for 50 years. His eldest son was Edward of Woodstock, also known as the Black Prince. He was never referred to as the Black Prince in his lifetime and there is debate over the origin of the sobriquet. Some believe that he wore a black suit of armour or at least a black cuirass (chest plate). Others claim that it was a French nickname given to the prince for his savagery and cruelty.

The Black Prince was born at Woodstock Palace in Oxfordshire, later to become the site of Blenheim Palace. He inherited the title of Prince of Wales and was created Duke of Cornwall (the first ever British duke). The two titles have continued to be given to a reigning monarch's eldest son. The current holder is Prince Charles. When and if he becomes King Charles III, Prince William will inherit the titles.

Prince Charles has visited Romania several times since the 1980s, when under the rule of communist dictator Nicolae Ceauşescu, villages were destroyed to move farmers to apartment buildings in cities. The prince has shown great personal interest in the fate of the Saxon villages of Transylvania.

Irish writer Abraham 'Bram' Stoker (1847–1912) chose Transylvania as the setting for his 1897 novel *Dracula*, having found a kind of gory inspiration in the figure of Vlad the Impaler.

Vlad III the Impaler or Vlad Ţepeş or Vlad Dracula or Vlad Drăculea was a prince of Wallachia, now part of Romania. He reigned briefly in 1448, from 1456 to 1462, and again briefly in 1476. Vlad was famed for his cruelty. He drove nails into people's heads, cut off their limbs, blinded them, strangled them and burned them. He regularly cut off noses and ears, mutilated sexual organs, skinned people and boiled them alive. But he is most famous for his preferred method of torture and execution – impalement on sharpened wooden stakes. Some people took days to die and the corpses were often left decaying for months as an example to any who would oppose him.

A famous woodcut shows Vlad feasting amongst a forest of impaled people. This depicts the notorious incident in 1459 when he had 30,000 people from the city of Braşov – men, women and children – impaled on Saint Bartholomew's Day.

St Bartholomew was one of the twelve Apostles of Jesus. His name means son of Ptolemy (Ptolemy was a Greek mathematician, astronomer and geographer who was, curiously, born in the year AD 101). In works of art St Bartholomew is often shown holding a knife and in Michelangelo's *Last Judgement*, he is shown with his own skin hanging over his arm. This is because tradition holds that he was flayed alive and then crucified upside down. This fate has led to him being adopted as the patron saint of tanners.

Tanning is the process of converting animal skin into leather. The name comes from the use of tannin – an acidic compound – which preserves the skin and prevents decomposition. These days the whole process is done with chemicals but in past times the procedure was far more disgusting.

Skins arrived at the tannery dried stiff and often had rotting fat, blood and hair attached. The skins were scraped, scoured and soaked in stale urine. Then, once the hair was removed, the tanners would pound dung into the skin or soak them in a solution made of liquidized animal brains. Pots were left around the local area for people to provide the urine and children were employed as dung gatherers.

Skinning animals and using their hides as leather or

fur was the main plot line of Dodie Smith's 1956 novel *The Hundred and One Dalmatians*. Subtitled *The Great Dog Robbery*, it tells the story of evil socialite Cruella de Vil's attempt to make a coat out of Dalmatian puppy skins. A sequel entitled *The Starlight Barking* continues the first novel. It has been turned into both an animated and live action film by Walt Disney with a slight change of title to *101 Dalmatians*.

The tallest building in the world (at time of writing) is called Taipei 101 . . .

Round 15

BY JOVE! WHAT
THE DICKENS?

English artist Roger Dean created many of the iconic album covers of the 1970s. His curious mix of organic architecture, fantasy imagery and staggeringly complex and beautifully rendered typography gave us classic album covers and logos for bands like Yes, Osibisa, Budgie, Greenslade, Asia and Uriah Heep.

Uriah Heep was a character in *David Copperfield* by Charles Dickens. Charles Dickens was a clever man – clerk, court stenographer, journalist and campaigner against social injustice – but was once famously tricked by an eccentric Cornish vicar called the Reverend Robert Hawker.

Hawker became vicar of Morwenstow in Cornwall in 1834 and was in the post for over 40 years. He was a folklorist and poet and invented the harvest festival as we know it today. His 'The Song of the Western Men' has become the unofficial Cornish national anthem under the shorter, snappier name of 'Trelawny'.[20] Hawker wrote the poem 'under a stag-horned oak in Sir Beville's Walk in Stowe Wood' and sent it anonymously to a Plymouth newspaper claiming it to be a traditional song. It subsequently attracted favourable comments from Sir Walter Scott and Charles Dickens, who promoted it as a long-lost anthem.

Hawker loved bright colours and abhorred his religious clothes. It's said that the only black things he ever wore were his socks. He was often seen wearing a rich-plum-coloured coat, a blue fisherman's jersey, wellington boots and a pink brimless hat. He also set a new fashion by wearing a poncho made from a yellow horse blanket, which he claimed was the 'ancient habit of St Pardarn'. He was often accompanied on his meanderings by his pet, an enormous pig.

He talked to birds. He is known to have dressed up as a mermaid for fun. He invited his nine cats to church services but excommunicated one of them for

20 Sir Jonathan Trelawny (1650–1721), a Cornishman and Bishop of Bristol, was one of seven bishops imprisoned in the Tower of London by James II in 1687 for 'seditious libel'. The staunchly Protestant Cornish were very vocal in his defence. His name is often misspelled as Trelawney.

mousing on a Sunday. He was a regular opium smoker and often wrote poetry while under the influence. He built himself a driftwood hut high up on the cliffs and spent many hours inside, smoking and writing his poems and keeping his eye on the sea. This hut is now the smallest property owned by the National Trust.

The National Trust was founded in 1895 by three Victorian philanthropists – Sir Robert Hunter, Canon Hardwicke Rawnsley and Miss Octavia Hill – concerned that uncontrolled urbanization and industrialization were destroying the countryside they loved. So they bought big chunks of it to keep it safe.

Octavia Hill (born 1838) and her sister Miranda (born 1836) were the granddaughters of Dr Thomas Southwood Smith, a pioneer of sanitary reform. Southwood Smith (1788–1861) was a doctor from Somerset who became the first person to find a direct connection between epidemic illness and poverty. He became a bit of an epidemics expert and was frequently consulted by public authorities. He achieved international recognition for his studies on fighting cholera and yellow fever.

Yellow fever is a dangerous tropical illness transmitted by the domestic mosquito (*Stegomyia fasciata*). Mosquitoes are essentially nectar feeders. However, the females of most species also require meals of blood in order to reproduce. Hence all that irritating biting nonsense.

The de Havilland Mosquito was one of the most successful combat aircraft of the Second World War. The aircraft was made mostly from wood as the company had the foresight to realize that metal would become scarcer as the war went on. They also realized that traditional woodworkers, such as furniture makers (around 5,000 of the total 7,781 Mosquitoes ever made contained parts made in High Wycombe, Bucking-hamshire, a town that was once the centre of UK furniture production and which even has a chair museum to this day), could be retrained very quickly for aircraft production. Almost the entire plane was built of plywood, balsa and spruce. The total weight of metal components used in the aircraft was just 280 pounds.

The Mosquito flew for the first time on 25 November 1940. The designers believed that it would be able to travel at least 20 mph faster than the Supermarine Spitfire. In the end, the Mosquito exceeded all expectations and its twin Rolls-Royce Merlin 25 engines and light weight allowed the plane to achieve a top speed of 361 knots (415 mph) at 28,000 feet. The top speed of the Spitfire was 330 knots (378 mph). The Mosquito was the fastest aircraft in Bomber Command until May 1951. From this point on, all speed records would be held by jets.

A comparable aeroplane was the Bristol Blenheim. When Britain went to war in 1939 the Blenheim was undoubtedly the most important aircraft in the Royal Air Force, being the fastest bomber and heavy fighter around with a top speed of 231 knots (266 mph). But, in a curiously ironic twist, the plane that helped the British win the war had a German name.

The aircraft was named after Blenheim Palace, seat of the Duke of Marlborough and birthplace of Winston Churchill. However, the palace is itself named after a town in Bavaria – the largest and oldest state in Germany – where the first Duke of Marlborough won a decisive victory against Louis XIV in 1704. As a reward, Queen Anne gave the Royal Manor of Woodstock to John Churchill and paid for the grand Palace of Blenheim, as she called it, to be built.

The Blenheim aircraft was designed by Bristol's chief designer Frank Barnwell, who, back in 1915, had designed one of the outstanding military planes of World War I, the Bristol Fighter. This was an extremely agile and well-armed two-seater biplane and was the aircraft piloted by Victoria Cross winner William Leefe Robinson when he took on Manfred von Richthofen, the so-called Red Baron. The Bristol Fighter (or F2) was powered by engines made by Rolls-Royce, but once the war ended, Bristol began making their own. The most successful engine they produced was the Bristol Jupiter, which stayed in production from 1918 to 1930.

Jupiter means Father Jove in Latin and was the title accorded in classical mythology to the king of the gods. His Greek equivalent was Zeus.

Jupiter is also the name of a town in Florida, USA. It takes its name from the Spanish name of the original residents, the Jobe (properly pronounced as 'ho-bay'), which was anglicized to Jove and, ultimately, morphed into Jupiter. The local minor league baseball team is the Jupiter Hammerheads, an affiliate of the state team, the Florida Marlins. The Jupiter Hammerheads are based at the Roger Dean Stadium in Jupiter.

English artist Roger Dean created many of the iconic album covers of the 1970s . . .

FASCISTS, FIRST FLIGHTS AND FRAT PACKS

During World War II the Nazis considered forcibly relocating the entire European population of Jews to the then French-owned island of Madagascar, off the east coast of Africa. The Madagascar Plan depended on the imminent victory in France (as a result of which all of its colonies would come under German control) and the belief that Great Britain would be the next to fall. The plan even envisioned using the captured Royal Navy to effect the evacuation. The plan was abandoned in favour of the loathsome Jewish 'super-ghettoes', which ultimately became the death camps.

The Nazis exterminated some six million Jews but also murdered around two million non-Jewish Poles, 800,000 Roma and Sinti (Gypsies), 300,000 people with physical and/or mental disabilities, 200,000 Freemasons, 100,000 communists, 25,000 homosexual men and 5,000 Jehovah's Witnesses. In addition, they killed six million other Slavic civilians, four million Soviet prisoners of war and 1.5 million political dissidents.

The horrible mechanical efficiency of the Holocaust was supported by the SS and German army, but also by police units under the control of the Nazis during the war. Reserve Police Battalion 101 alone allegedly shot 38,000 Jews and deported 45,000 more to the extermination camps in just one year. And even private firms helped. Sympathizers at the Paris branch of Barclays Bank volunteered the names of Jewish employees to the authorities, and many of these ended up in the death camps. And there are allegations that an early incarnation of the company that would become IBM designed the Hollerith punch card technology that the Nazis used to identify and catalogue the prisoners ... although they would probably not have been aware of the terrible use their technology was being put to.

IBM stands for International Business Machines. The original name of the company was the Computing Tabulating Recording Company or CTR Co. But soon the range and scope of the company necessitated a change of name. So, on 14 February 1924, after just 13 years in business, CTR formally became the International Business Machines Corporation.

During the filming of Arthur C. Clarke and Stanley Kubrick's *2001 A Space Odyssey*, IBM contributed advice about computers and how they saw them developing in the future. However, once they discovered that the computer – named Athena in early scripts – was going to go mad and kill people, they insisted on all IBM logos being removed. The story goes that Kubrick and Clarke were less than pleased with this and therefore displaced the letters of IBM by one character to create the name of the dysfunctional murdering HAL9000 computer. However Kubrick later stated that it was just a coincidence. Clarke went one further, claiming that HAL actually stood for Heuristically Programmed Algorithmic Computer. He even wrote to the computer magazine *Byte* to place his denial on record. It's interesting that Clarke's and Kubrick's stories differ and that Clarke's version of events actually creates the acronym HPAC rather than HAL.

An acronym is a word usually made from the initial letters of a title or name or phrase. The word comes from Greek, meaning heads of names. Well-known examples include AWOL (absent without leave), NATO (North Atlantic Treaty Organization), RADAR (radio detection and ranging) and LASER (light amplification by stimulated emissions of radiation). It's a relatively new phenomenon and all acronyms date from the twentieth century. This doesn't stop people inventing all sorts of nonsense about the origins of older phrases. For instance, POSH does not come from Port out starboard home and GOLF does not mean Gentlemen only ladies forbidden. These retro-engineered acronyms have been termed 'backronyms'.

Extraordinarily, the term IOU is not a shortening of I owe you but a true acronym of is owed unto. IOU is also the Interdependent Occupational Unit, the currency of writer and broadcaster Danny Wallace's micro-nation of Lovely. For his BBC TV series *How to Start Your Own Country* Wallace declared his flat in Bow, East London, an independent (and doubleglazed) country and invited people to become his citizens. Although entirely silly in its premise, the show did demonstrate the difficulties that exist in forming a new nation. One of Wallace's other projects, the best-selling book *Yes Man*, told the story of what happened when he decided to say yes to every question he was asked. The book has been turned into a feature film starring Jim Carrey in the lead role. Originally Jack Black was put forward as the likely star. Black appeared with Carrey in the 1996 film *The Cable Guy*, as did Owen Wilson and Ben Stiller (who also directed the film).

Jack Black is a member of the Hollywood Frat Pack, which includes Ben Stiller, Will Ferrell, Vince Vaughn, and Owen and Luke Wilson. Owen and Luke Wilson played Wilbur and Orville Wright in the Jackie Chan/Steve Coogan film *Around the World in 80 Days*.

The Wright Brothers are generally credited with making the first controlled, powered, heavier-than-air human flight on 17 December 1903. Bizarrely, the first exclusive eye-witness report of the historic manned flight was published in the magazine *Gleanings in Bee Culture*.

The Wright Brothers' place in history is disputed almost as much as the whole IBM/HAL story. For example, John Stringfellow (1799–1883), a bobbin maker for the lace industry, spent many years working on the Aerial Steam Carriage with William Samuel Henson, with whom he shared the vision of creating an international company, the Aerial Transit Company.

While their designs were flawed, they did achieve the first powered flight in 1848, when their ten-foot-long steam-driven flying machine successfully flew the length of a disused lace factory in Chard, Somerset.

Chard (*Beta vulgaris*) is a cultivated form of wild sea beet. Sugar beet (another variety of *Beta vulgaris*) contains a high concentration of sucrose and is therefore grown commercially for sugar. France and Germany lead the world in terms of volume, producing approximately 30 million tons each per year. The European beet sugar industry really took off during the Napoleonic Wars when the British blockade of France prevented the import of cane sugar from the Caribbean.

The production of sugar beet was a major fundraiser for the Nazi war effort. The Nazis – the name short for Nationalsozialistische Deutsche Arbeiterpartei (National Socialist German Workers Party or NSDAP) – took control of the sugar beet farms in France, Italy and Poland and worked them with prisoners of war as slave labour.

During World War II the Nazis considered forcibly relocating the entire European population of Jews . . .

Round 17

IF AT FIRST YOU
DON'T SUCCEED . . .
HAVE AN APPLE

Kenning is a poetic device that comes from the old Norse phrase *kenna eitt við* (to express a thing in terms of another). So instead of calling the sea 'the sea', the kenning Norseman would call it a whale-way. Or a comb a bug rake. Milk becomes cow juice. Beer becomes fighter fuel.

There are hundreds of thousands of different 'fighter fuels' brewed around the world, and there are as many surprising names as there are flavours. Among them are Old Engine Oil, Blithering Idiot, Seriously Bad Elf, Dragon's Milk Oak Barrel Ale, Pig's Ass Porter, Stumblin' Monk, Moose Drool, My Old Kentucky Homo, Arrogant Bastard, Dead Frog, Sick Duck, Collaborator Hallucinator Old Ale, Nude Ale, Choco-

Bear, Pliny the Younger, La Fin du Monde (The End of the World) and Dead Armadillo.

The armadillo (*Dasypus novemcinctus*) is the only animal, besides humans and mice, which can contract leprosy. In a series of tests in Texas and Louisiana during 1985 between 2 and 5 per cent of wild armadillos were found to be harbouring the leprosy bacterium.

Leprosy, more properly called Hansen's disease, is an infectious disease carried within the *leprae* mycobacterium. There are an estimated 15 million victims around the world, mostly in the tropics. The USA has around 3000 known victims. It affects the skin, nerves and mucous membranes causing disfigurement, paralysis and the degeneration of tissues. Famous lepers include the nineteenth-century Brazilian sculptor Aleijadinho, King Henry VII of Germany and Robert the Bruce of Scotland. Evidence of the latter was found when the Bruce's skull was examined and found to be missing the canine teeth, a common skeletal sign of leprosy.

Robert the Bruce (or Robert de Brus) was born on 11 July 1274, the eldest son of Robert de Brus, 6th Lord of Annandale, and Marjorie, Countess of Carrick, daughter of Niall, Earl of Carrick. He went on to become King of Scotland, leading his countrymen to independence from the English.

He was crowned Robert I, King of Scots, at Scone near Perth, on 25 March 1306. He claimed the throne by way of being the great-great-great-great-grandson of David I of Scotland. It took him a while to assemble a kingdom and he suffered a number of defeats in battle against Edward I of England. However, upon Edward's death in 1307 Robert took advantage of the changeover to attack the weaker King Edward II's armies. Over the next eight years Robert waged a guerrilla war against the English, culminating in the Battle of Bannockburn in 1314. The English defeated, Scotland's armies could now invade northern England and Ireland. Robert the Bruce envisaged a pan-Gaelic greater Scotia with his bloodline ruling over both Ireland and Scotland. His marriage into the de Burgh family of Ulster helped, as did the fact that Robert's mother was a Carrick, descended from Gaelic royalty.

The most famous story about Robert the Bruce concerns a spider. After his defeat at Methven in 1306 and the subsequent rout of his forces, he hid in a cave near Gretna. While in the cave, he watched a spider trying to spin a web. Each time the spider failed, it simply started all over again. Inspired by this 'If at first you don't succeed, try and try again' attitude, Robert rallied his army and eventually defeated his enemy. Sadly, the story is almost certainly untrue as it first appears in Sir Walter Scott's *Tales of a Grandfather*, published in 1828 nearly 500 years after Robert's death.

Robert the Bruce died on 7 June 1329, at the Manor of Cardross, Dunbarton. He is recorded as having died of an 'unclean ailment'. This may have been syphilis, psoriasis, or a series of strokes (leprosy may not have been the actual cause of death). His body is buried in Dunfermline Abbey, but his heart was taken on a crusade to the Holy Land by Sir James Douglas. It only made it as far as Spain, where Douglas was killed. Legend says that it was then returned to Scotland and interred at Melrose Abbey.

Among the many Scottish clans that supported Robert the Bruce, we find the Shaw, Robertson, Seton, Sinclair and Mackintosh clans. The name Mackintosh or MacIntosh derives from the Gaelic *mac-an-toiseach* and means son of the chief.

The Macintosh computer is not named after a Scotsman but a species of apple. The Apple company itself was named after co-founder Steve Jobs' favourite fruit (at one time he worked in an orchard). The story goes that he was close to the deadline for registering his new company and plucked the name out of the air. He then told his colleagues that unless they could think of anything better by 5 p.m. that day, that would be it. They didn't and it was. Jobs and crew weren't that displeased with this choice as they'd wanted a company name that sounded more friendly than the rather abrupt names of other computer companies such as IBM, NEC, Dylakor, Tesseract and Synscort.

When it was time to give Apple's new computer a name, engineer Jeff Raskin chose the name McIntosh after a particular species of apple. The McIntosh Red apple is unique in that every single apple can be traced back to a single tree discovered in 1796 by John McIntosh on his farm in Dundela, Ontario. Raskin felt that this was an appropriate name for the new computer as it complemented the Apple name and because he believed that every future computer would have a traceable lineage back to the first Apple Mac. However, use of the name McIntosh proved to be a problem as it was already in use by an upmarket audio manufacturing company. Apple eventually paid a one-time royalty of $100,000 to McIntosh Laboratory, Inc., and changed their spelling to the variant Macintosh.

Current generations of Macintosh hardware have the prefix i (iMac, iPhone, etc.) as does Apple's bestselling portable music player, the iPod. There has been some debate about what the i stands for. Writer Greg Crosby claimed that iPod was an acronym of 'interface protocol option device', but this turned out to be a 'backronym' practical joke, as did other derivations such as 'I pay online devotedly' and 'Idiots price our devices'. A number of people have even suggested that the i in iPod stands for isolation. In fact, it simply stands for Internet as it was used as the prefix for the first Internet-ready Mac. The i has since become part of Apple's brand identity.

Apples, along with other fruits, oilseeds, vegetables, coal, hair and grain, used to be measured in bushels. An imperial bushel is defined as eight imperial gallons. As a measurement, it is slowly disappearing as it is replaced by standard metric units.

A quarter of a bushel is called a peck (as immortalized in the tongue-twister 'Peter Piper picked a peck of pickled pepper'). Two pecks or half a bushel is called a kenning.

Kenning is a poetic device that comes from . . .

MURDER MOST NUCLEAR

Margaret Rutherford DBE (1892–1972) was an Academy Award-winning English character actress best known for her appearances as Agatha Christie's Miss Marple in a series of films made during the early 1960s. They were: *Murder, She Said* (1961), *Murder at the Gallop* (1963), *Murder Most Foul* (1964) and *Murder Ahoy!* (1964). The films also all featured Charles 'Bud' Tingwell as Inspector Craddock and Stringer Davis (Rutherford's real-life husband) as Mr Stringer.

Her father, William Rutherford Benn, suffered from mental illness for many years and on 4 March 1883 murdered his own father, the Reverend Julius Benn, by battering him to death with a chamber pot. He spent the rest of his life in Broadmoor maximum security prison.

Dame Margaret Rutherford was a cousin of the left-wing Labour politician Tony Benn.

Mr Benn was a 1970s animated children's TV series narrated by actor Ray Brooks. A dapper man in a pinstriped suit and bowler hat, Mr Benn would visit a local costume shop to try on a new outfit every episode. However, when he stepped out of the changing room door, he would find himself in another world where his costume would be appropriate – for example, he would put on an astronaut suit and walk out into a space adventure. Based on the books by writer and artist David McKee, there were originally 13 episodes with a fourteenth ('Mr Benn the Gladiator') made in 2005 for the Nickelodeon channel. As we were told in the introduction of every episode, Mr Benn lived at number 52 Festive Road. This was based on a real street, Festing Road in Putney, London, where David McKee used to live.

Putney is in south-west London in the Borough of Wandsworth. It was the site of firstly a Roman settlement and then an Anglo Saxon one named Putta's Landing, Putta presumably being the name of a local chieftain. Throughout history the name has gone through a number of mutations including Putelei (eleventh century), Poultenheth, Pultynghyde (fourteenth century), Potenhith, Pottenhith (fifteenth century), Putenega, Putneythe, Puttennethe, Potney (sixteenth

century) and Pottnie and Puttney (seventeenth century). Putney Bridge marks the starting point of the
annual Oxford and Cambridge Boat Race, and Charles
Dickens made Putney Church the setting for David
Copperfield's marriage to Dora Spenlow.

David Copperfield is the stage name of the magician
David Seth Kotkin. During his highly successful career
Copperfield has made the Statue of Liberty disappear,
apparently impaled himself on a sword, appeared to fly
and walked through the Great Wall of China.

The Great Wall of China is the world's longest
man-made structure, stretching 3,948 miles from Shan-
hai Pass to Lop Nur. Along most of its length it
roughly marks the border between China and Mongo-
lia. Contrary to popular misconceptions, you cannot
see the Great Wall of China from space. However, it
can be seen from a close Earth orbit . . . but it is then
no more visible than any other large man-made structure such as roads, canals or oilfields.

In June 1899 a number of US newspapers published
a story about bids by American businesses to demolish
the Great Wall and construct a road in its place. It
turned out to be a hoax perpetrated by four Denver
newspaper reporters, Al Stevens, Jack Tournay, John
Lewis and Hal Wilshire when they had nothing else to

write about. The story soon spread across the USA and on to China where, so the story goes, it contributed to the Boxer Rebellion. However, the rebellion had already started before the Great Wall hoax was perpetrated and as there is no reference to it in any Chinese history of the era, this is probably an urban myth.

Throughout the nineteenth century China's emperors had watched in horror as various foreign powers had slowly but surely undermined their rule. With every new concession made to the West, Tsu Hsi, empress dowager of the Ch'ing dynasty, became angrier and she swore to find a way to get rid of the foreigners once and for all. Meanwhile, a severe drought was devastating northern Shandong province and a militant group called the Righteous Harmony Society was getting hot under the collar about the lack of government action. There was even talk of rebellion and the overthrow of the Ch'ings, something that would have worried the empress dowager as Society members were known to be highly trained in the martial arts and also believed that they had magical powers – to the extent that they claimed that bullets would not harm them.

Tsu Hsi succeeded in deflecting the Righteous Harmony Society's fury towards the 'foreign devils'. Crafty manipulation and clever use of disinformation soon had the Society chanting slogans like 'Support the Ch'ing; destroy the foreigner!' and in early 1900 thousands of the Society's members started roaming the countryside, attacking and killing Christian missionaries. As they moved towards the larger towns and cities, their numbers grew as more disaffected peasants joined the Society. By the time they entered Beijing, the rebellious army was some 20,000 strong. Then began a siege of the foreign embassies that lasted two months. Messages were sent to their home countries demanding help, which eventually came in the form of soldiers and sailors from eight countries. The Western army then looted the capital and the empress dowager, disguised as a peasant, was forced to escape the city in a cart. The power of the Ch'ing dynasty was destroyed and the new rulers of China agreed to a more 'open door' policy with the West, protecting Chinese interests while also allowing free trade.

These events became known as the Boxer Rebellion due to a mistranslation. The Righteous Harmony

Society was wrongly dubbed the Fists of Righteous Harmony by Western translators and quickly gained the nickname 'Boxers' as a result.

'The Boxer' is one of Simon and Garfunkel's most popular songs and appeared on the duo's swan-song album *Bridge Over Troubled Water* in 1970. Paul Simon wrote the song in 1968 and claims that it is largely autobiographical: 'I think the song was about me,' he said. 'Everybody's beating me up'.

The name USS *Boxer* has been given to six ships of the United States Navy. The fifth was an aircraft carrier launched in 1944 and decommissioned in 1971. On 10 March 1948 USS *Boxer* was the first ship to ever land a jet aircraft (an FJ-1 Fury) on its deck.

One jet aircraft that could never have landed on the USS *Boxer* is the B52 Stratofortress. At 159 feet long, 40 feet 8 inches high and with a massive wingspan of 185 feet, the Stratofortress is one of the largest aircraft to have ever flown.

The B52 gave its name to a hairstyle popular in the 1950s that resembled the shape of the airplane's nose section. In turn, the hairstyle gave its name to the American band that scored big hits with 'Rock Lobster', 'Love Shack' and 'Roam' in the 1980s and 1990s. The B52s made a cameo appearance in the 1994 live action film *The Flintstones* as 'rock' band the BC52s. The film was received reasonably well and grossed over $130 million in America alone. The one moan that most critics and fans had was the casting of Rosie O'Donnell as Betty Rubble. Although she had mastered most of Betty's mannerisms and played the character well, her build certainly did not mirror the svelte form of Ms Rubble as seen in the original cartoon series. Perhaps in consequence of this, O'Donnell was the unfair recipient of a Razzie Award for worst supporting actress for the film.

In the same year Paul Simon wrote 'The Boxer' a B52 carrying four nuclear bombs crashed in Greenland, causing widespread panic. It happened on 28 January and took 700 men over nine months to remove all the contaminated material, including snow, from the crash site. America subsequently ended the airborne alert which kept some B52 bombers in the air at all times in case of surprise nuclear attack. They were finally taken off 'alert duty' in 1991 by President George H. W. Bush. Despite being officially replaced by the XB70 Valkyrie, the B1 Lancer and the B2 Spirit stealth bomber, the B52 is still in service and may continue to be so for a further twenty-odd years.

The B52 can cruise at high subsonic speeds at

altitudes up to 50,000 feet and fly up to 12,000 miles. It was originally designed as a deterrent during the Cold War, staying in the air with its atomic payload, which could be delivered to any point in the USSR.

The atomic bomb works by nuclear fission. This is the process of splitting the nucleus of an atom apart. When this is done, a tremendous amount of energy – both heat and light – is released. When an atom splits it releases neutrons, which under the right conditions go on to split other atoms in a chain reaction. If each splitting atom causes one released neutron to split another atom, it's called a critical chain reaction and this creates a steady release of heat energy (as used in nuclear power stations). But if each fission releases two or more neutrons that go on to split other atoms, the chain reaction becomes supercritical and rapidly cascades into an almost instantaneous, massive, explosive release of energy.

The father of modern nuclear physics was a New Zealand professor called Ernest Rutherford (1871–1937) who was the first to show that the atom was made of smaller particles. He also gave us the terms nucleus, half-life, and alpha, beta and gamma ray. He received the Nobel Prize in 1908 and was knighted in 1914. The atom was first split, by a team under his direction, in 1932, using a particle accelerator. Having done this, Rutherford famously said, 'The energy produced by the atom is a very poor kind of thing. Anyone who expects a source of power from the transformation of these atoms is talking moonshine.'

In 1945 the nuclear bomb 'Little Boy' was dropped on the Japanese city of Hiroshima. This 'very poor kind of thing' instantly killed an estimated 70,000–80,000 people and caused total destruction across one square mile, with resulting fires across 4.4 square miles.

Rutherford's ashes are buried in the nave of Westminster Abbey, near the tombs of Sir Isaac Newton and Lord Kelvin.

Although there are a number of theories about the origin of the name Rutherford, it is likely to have come from the Borders region of Scotland (Ernest Rutherford's father was originally from Perth, Scotland). The name has since spread and mutated, becoming Rhetorfortis, Routherfurd, Ruderford, Rudderfoord and the delicious Ritterfart. But all can be traced back to the ancestral family, as noted by K. Rutherford Davis: 'Every person with a Rutherford ancestry by blood is descended from the medieval lairds of Rutherford.'[21] Therefore, in some remote way Ernest Rutherford would have been related to other famous Rutherfords including Mike Rutherford of Genesis, Thomas Rutherford, the 'Black Laird of Edgerston', who defeated the English during the Battle of the Red Swire in July 1575, and actress Dame Margaret Rutherford.

Margaret Rutherford DBE . . .

---

21 *The Rutherfords in Britain: A history and guide*, Alan Sutton, Gloucester, 1987.

GO, GO POWER HOSTAGE!

It is possible to hypnotize a chicken. You hold its head against the ground and draw a line starting at its beak and extending straight out in front of the chicken. You keep doing this over and over again until the chicken becomes immobile. It will then stay like this for between 15 seconds and 30 minutes. Iggy Pop mentions this in the lyrics to his hit 'Lust for Life':

> *I've been hurting since I've bought the gimmick*
> *About something called love*
> *Yeah, something called love.*
> *Well, that's like hypnotizing chickens.*

Iggy Pop – real name James Newell Osterberg Jr – got his stage name from being lead singer of a band called the Iguanas in his youth. He later formed the Stooges but his ever-growing drug problems pulled the band apart. His career was rescued by David Bowie, who helped write and produced *The Idiot* and *Lust for Life* (both 1977), Pop's two most acclaimed albums as a solo artist.

Iggy Pop appeared as an actor in John Waters' 1990 cult musical *Cry-Baby*. The spoof 1950s teen movie featured an eclectic cast led by Johnny Depp and Amy Locane. Others in the film included porn star Traci Lords, chat-show host Ricki Lake and heiress turned kidnap victim turned bank-robbing terrorist turned actress Patti Hearst.

Hearst, granddaughter of newspaper magnate William Randolph Hearst, was kidnapped from her apartment in 1974 by an urban guerrilla group calling itself the Symbionese Liberation Army. She was just 19 at the time. Initially, the SLA tried to swap Hearst for jailed members of their group. When this failed, they forced the Hearst family to cough up $6 million worth of food, which was distributed to the poor. However, Hearst was still not released and her family feared the worst . . . until she was seen and photographed carrying an assault rifle while robbing a bank in San Francisco. In subsequent communications she adopted the pseudonym of Tania and revealed that she had joined the SLA. A year later she was arrested, along with other members of the gang.

At her trial Hearst claimed that she had been coerced into joining the gang by a form of brainwashing involving physical and sexual abuse. However, it has also been suggested that she had a severe case of Stockholm syndrome.

Stockholm syndrome is a psychological response to a situation of danger and entrapment in which the victim starts to feel sympathy for their captor(s). In extreme cases the victim befriends the captor and even defends their actions. The term was coined by the criminologist and psychiatrist Nils Bejerot after an incident in August 1973 when bank robbers held staff at the Kreditbanken in Normalmstorg, Stockholm, Sweden as hostages for six days. When the hostages were finally freed, they did not want to press charges and offered to act as witnesses for the defence.

'Stockholm Syndrome' is also the name of a song recorded by UK rock band Muse. It appears on their third studio album *Absolution*. Muse lyrics feature references to such subjects as global conspiracy, extra-terrestrial life, terrorism, psychological disorder, theology and the Apocalypse. On their most recent album,

Black Holes and Revelations, the band's fascination with the Book of Revelation and the Four Horsemen of the Apocalypse is very evident, as is their interest in Mars, in particular the region of Cydonia.

Cydonia aroused international interest when in July 1975 the US *Viking* spacecraft photographed the area from orbit. It is a vast plain dotted with mesas, but one stood out from the others as it appeared uncannily like a human face, albeit without a nose. The 'face on Mars' attracted all kinds of theories including that it was evidence of a once-mighty Martian culture and this was their equivalent of the Great Pyramids or Sphinx at Giza in Egypt. Unfortunately, recent high-definition photographs have shown that there is no face. It was an optical illusion caused by the very-low-definition digital photography (820 feet per pixel) used at the time.

The Martian 'Sphinx' had no nose . . . and nor does the Earth's. Legend has it that the nose was destroyed by a cannonball fired by Napoleon's troops but sketches of the Sphinx from over 100 years earlier show the figure without its nasal appendage. The most likely account of its disappearance comes from the writings of fifteenth-century Egyptian historian al-Maqrizi, who claims that the statue was vandalized in

1378 by a chap called Sa'im al-Dahr who took umbrage when he saw peasants making offerings to the Sphinx in the hope of increasing the harvest. It is not known why this simple act upset him so much. It may be because, as a pagan act, it upset his orthodox Muslim sensibilities.

The Sphinx at Giza is the largest single-stone statue in the world. The figure, a lion with the head of a man, was carved out of the surrounding limestone bedrock and is 260 feet long, 20 feet wide and 65 feet high.

King Sphinx was a monster that threatened Earth in the first season of Japanese/US crossover series *Mighty Morphin Power Rangers*. *Power Rangers*, or *Kyouryuu Sentai Zyuranger* (Japanese Super Sentai), had already run for 16 successful seasons in Japan when it was decided to try to break into the lucrative American TV market. New scenes were shot using American teenagers and these were interspersed with the original Japanese footage, suitably dubbed into English. Usefully, the Japanese sequences had the Power Rangers in costumes that disguised the actors' features. The show also boasted a host of monsters in heavy costume.

King Sphinx could make people disappear using his

wings and fired flaming question marks from his gold sceptre. Among the other creatures the Power Rangers faced were the amusingly named Mr Ticklesneezer, Eye Guy, Pineoctopus, Samurai Fan Man, Robogoat, Grumble Bee, Pumpkin Rapper, Turkey Jerk, Oyster-izer, Adrian (?) and Chunky Chicken.

It is possible to hypnotize a chicken . . .

WAY OUT WEST
... IN WALES?
WAY OUT, MAN!

The Green Man is a term first coined by Lady Raglan in 1939 in her article 'The Green Man in Church Architecture', published in the *Folklore Journal*.

The Green Man refers specifically to a mythological character found in the UK, usually in the form of stone or wood carvings on religious buildings. The carvings range from a man's face peering out of foliage to extraordinary forms where the face is actually made of leaves and greenery and plant features emerge from various orifices. The original Green Man was probably a pagan figure – like the Woodwose (the hairy man of the woods), Jack in the Green, John Barleycorn and Robin Goodfellow, all of which are physical embodiments of the natural world – Earth spirits if you like.

There may also be links or parallels with other mythological characters such as the Green Knight, Herne the Hunter, the Horned God, Puck and even Robin Hood.

The first cinematic version of the Robin Hood story was made in 1922 and was silent. *Douglas Fairbanks in Robin Hood* (to give it its full and slightly odd title) was the first ever film to have a Hollywood premiere.

Fairbanks' portrayal of Robin Hood and that other great champion of the poor Zorro were major influences on Batman, according to creator Bob Kane. And the Batman–Robin Hood links don't end there . . . Batman's sidekick, Robin, first appeared in DC Comics in 1940, a year after Batman's debut. When artist Bob Kane and writer Jerry Robinson were designing the character, Robinson remembered some illustrations of Robin Hood by N. C. Wyeth. Consequently, Robin's original costume was given a kind of medieval look. As Robinson himself explains, 'I suggested [the name] Robin, which they seemed to like, and then showed them [my sketch of] the costume. And if you look at it, it's Wyeth's costume, from my memory.'

The place that Batman patrols and cares for is Gotham City, which is closely modelled on New York. 'Gotham City' was coined by writer Washington Irving in the early 1800s as a nickname for New York.

He intended it to mean 'city of fools' and his reasoning for this came from English folklore and the story of the Wise Men of Gotham. These were the inhabitants of the village of Gotham in Nottinghamshire – Robin Hood's home county – whose legendary stupidity was captured in a series of popular humorous fables and the nursery rhyme:

> *Three wise men of Gotham*
> *Went to sea in a bowl.*
> *If the bowl had been stronger*
> *My tale had been longer.*

Among their supposed exploits were forming a circle of people around a bush to keep a cuckoo there all summer, cutting a notch on the side of a boat to show where they'd hidden a church bell underwater, and trying to catch the Moon (reflected in a pond) in a net. However, the Wise Men may not have been so stupid after all. The tales are said to stem from an incident in which the villagers of Gotham feigned imbecility to frighten the hated King John away from living in the area.

John inherited the throne in 1199 upon the death of his big brother Richard I (the Lionheart). Until this time he had acted as a caretaker king while Richard had been off fighting in the Third Crusade. Unpopular as Prince John, he was even more so as king, and during his reign he upset the commoners, the nobles and even the Pope to such an extent that he was eventually forced to sign the Magna Carta in 1215, much against his will. For the first time this gave his subjects some legal rights. Robin Hood would have been pleased, having spent years cocking a snook at the man.

Douglas Fairbanks in Robin Hood cost around $1 million to make (one of the most expensive films ever made at the time) and featured a full-scale medieval village set. Many of the sets were designed by Frank Lloyd Wright Jr – son of America's most influential architect and later to become an architect himself. Among his works are the famous 'shells' that grace the Hollywood Bowl. The film was produced by Fairbanks and distributed by United Artists, a company owned by Fairbanks, his wife Mary Pickford, D. W. Griffith and Charlie Chaplin.

Charlie Chaplin was born on 16 April 1889 in London. His parents were both music hall performers and separated when he was only three years old. Chaplin had little contact with his alcoholic father and lived with his schizophrenic mother and older half-brother, Sydney. In due course his mother became so disturbed that she was admitted to an asylum in Surrey and the Chaplin children were consigned to a workhouse. The brothers became very close, relying heavily upon each other and developing their natural stage talent.

Chaplin eventually became a clown in Fred Karno's Fun Factory slapstick comedy troupe and toured America from 1910 to 1912. On their next tour, starting late in 1912, Chaplin ended up sharing a boarding-house room with his understudy, another British member of the Fred Karno troupe called Arthur Stanley Jefferson. In 1913 Chaplin was spotted by film producer Mack Sennett, who hired him to work for his Keystone Film Company. Arthur Jefferson, meanwhile, had adopted a new stage name and got himself film roles with Hal Roach's studio. He appeared in several silent comedies with another of Roach's actors, Babe Hardy, and the chemistry between them was soon spotted by supervising director Leo McCarey, who suggested that they be teamed up. As Laurel and Hardy, the two actors went on to become arguably the best comedy double act of all time.

They carried on working until 1951, when they

made the shambolic *Atoll K* in France. (In the USA the film was released under the title of *Utopia*; in the UK it was issued under the title *Robinson Crusoeland*.) It had a poor script, low budget, and many of the cast and crew spoke different languages (but not English). Stan Laurel was ill with diabetes throughout filming (and looked it) and Oliver Hardy had a heart problem that affected his performance. It was a tragically poor swansong for the duo and, other than a stage tour, they did not perform again. Illness was to dog them until 1957 when Oliver Hardy died of cerebral thrombosis. He had suffered a massive paralysing stroke just a few months before. Contrary to popular belief, Hardy's weight was not a contributing factor. In fact, losing weight may have killed him. On his doctor's orders he took off too much weight too fast, going from some 23 to 10 stone in a matter of a few months. This weakened his constitution to the extent that he was unable to fight further illness. Stan Laurel never worked again despite numerous offers. He did a little writing but that was all. He died of a heart attack seven years later.

Laurel and Hardy's films have enjoyed worldwide success. In Italy they are known as Stallio e Ollio. In Germany they are Dick und Doof (Fatty and Stupid).

In Spanish-speaking countries they are El Gordo y El Flaco (The Fat and the Thin). In Norway they are Helan og Halvan (The Whole and the Half) and the Polish call them Flip i Flap. In Portugal fans enjoy the comedy of Bucha e Estica (Chubby and Stretch) but my favourite is the Danish Gøg og Gokke, which sounds remarkably like the last three syllables of the Isle of Anglesey's most famous village and railway station at Llanfairpwllgwyngyllgogerychwyrndrobwlll-lantisiliogogogoch.

On road signs and Ordnance Survey maps the name is almost always recorded as Llanfairpwllgwyngyll. The extra bits were added in the nineteenth century in an attempt to generate tourism by having the longest place name in the UK. The full name translates as 'St Mary's church in the hollow of the white hazel near the rapid whirlpool and the church of St Tysilio of the red cave'.

The white hazel referred to in the place name is probably common witch hazel, which grows commonly around that part of Wales. Although originally from North America, the plant grows well in the UK and is a popular garden shrub with clusters of rich yellow to orange-red flowers. An extract made from the bark and leaves is used as an astringent and can be found in aftershave and lotions for treating bruises. The 'witch' part of the name has nothing to do with witches as it derives from the Old English *wice*, meaning bendy. The witch hazel is not closely related to the common hazel, from which we get hazelnuts and the pliable twigs used in dowsing.

The forked branch of a hazel tree used for dowsing is known as a *Virgula divina* or *Baculus divinatorius*. The dowser walks very slowly over where he or she believes there may be underground water or metal deposits. A mystical substance called effluvia – which dowsers claim is given off by the hidden metals or water – then enters the divining rod causing it to dip or twitch. Some dowsers also claim that they can access what Carl Jung called the collective unconscious or the superconscious mind by 'tuning into higher frequency vibrational planes of consciousness'. Other methods include meditation, clairvoyance, mediumship, remote viewing and the use of psychedelic drugs such as LSD, mescaline, cannabis and MDMA.

MDMA (methylenedioxymethamphetamine) is most commonly known by the street names Ecstasy, E, X, or XTC.

XTC is a British rock band from Swindon, Wiltshire. During the 1970s the band formed around songwriters Andy Partridge and Colin Moulding and multi-instrumentalist Dave Gregory. The band has had a troubled history and has frequently courted controversy. They stopped touring early in their career when frontman Partridge suffered a breakdown on stage. Their 1978 single 'Statue of Liberty' was banned from the air for its provocative lyrics about nakedness and looking up Liberty's skirt (they now seem very tame, but this was around the time of the Sex Pistols' 'God Save the Queen'). Their biggest hit, 1979's 'Making Plans for Nigel', also ruffled feathers by ironically referring to his 'future in British Steel' just as many of the nationalized industries were being run down with huge job losses. Most controversial of all was 1987's 'Dear God' in which a child sings the words of a letter to God asking why he allows terrible things to happen:

The wars you bring, the babes you drown, those lost
at sea and never found,
And it's the same the whole world round. The hurt I
see helps to compound
That the father, son and holy ghost, is just
somebody's unholy hoax,

*And if you're up there you'll perceive, that my heart's
    here upon my sleeve.
If there's one thing I don't believe in . . . It's you.*

In recent years the band has dissolved but their supposedly final album – the two-part *Apple Venus* (1999) and *Wasp Star* (2000) – is said by many to be their finest work. The tracklist includes songs like 'River of Orchids', 'Your Dictionary', 'I'm the Man Who Murdered Love', 'The Wheel and the Maypole' and 'Greenman'.

The Green Man is a term first coined . . .

IT'S AN
ASTRONOMICAL CON!

The Asteroid Belt is a huge circle of rocks and debris that orbits the Sun between Mars and Jupiter. It may be the result of a planet (hypothetically named Phaeton) that broke up billions of years ago, but is more commonly believed to be 'the planet that didn't happen'. The planets in our solar system were formed when gravity caused small rocks (or planetesimals) to crash together and slowly build in size like snowballs. It's thought that the gravity fields in the region between Mars and Jupiter attracted planetesimals but were not strong enough to allow the pieces to stick together. Consequently, the belt is composed of countless rocks, some the size of gravel to others the dimensions of a small planetoid.

It has been estimated that if all these asteroids were

crushed together into a ball, it would only be 4 per cent the mass of our Moon. The biggest asteroids account for much of that mass with the largest, Ceres at 600 miles across, contributing one third of the mass of the entire Asteroid Belt. Contrary to what you see in sci-fi films, the Asteroid Belt is very, very empty and the likelihood of hitting a rock by accident is minimal. Indeed, space probes such as the *Voyager* series have happily flown through and on to the outer planets without mishap.

Most of the asteroids are named after astronomers and scientists and authors and artists and places, but others are named after celebrities, modern cultural references and icons. Among these are:

Number 1569 Evita, 1629 Pecker, 1773 Rumpelstilz (after Rumpelstilzskin), 2303 Retsina, 2832 Lada, 2843 Yeti, 4386 Lüst, 5762 Wänke, 4629 Walford, 5805 Glasgow, 6000 United Nations and 9951 Tyrannosaurus. Asteroids 4147–50 are named after the Beatles and 9617–22 after members of Monty Python's Flying Circus. Most of the characters in Lewis Carroll's *Alice in Wonderland* are represented, with the Cheshire Cat being 6042, Mad Hatter 6735 and March Hare 6736. There are also asteroids named Marjorie (4064), Gary (4735), Nicky (4755) and Eric (4954).

Will future astronauts ever land on Eric? Who can say.

Asteroidal names are decided by the International Astronomical Union, which during 2006 was given the task of reclassifying the planets of our solar system. Until 2006 the solar system had officially consisted of nine planets. However, new discoveries had called into question the precise definition of what a planet is. As a result, Pluto was downgraded from planet to dwarf planet status and was joined by Ceres (formerly considered an asteroid) and Eris (a body beyond Pluto). The solar system therefore now consists of eight planets and three dwarf planets.

Eris was unnamed for some time (or at least only had its official registry names of 136199 or 2003 UB_{313}). It is the largest of the dwarf planets and is actually bigger than Pluto, which was one of the factors that led to the reclassification. Until it was officially named, the dwarf planet enjoyed the nickname of Xena, after the character played by Lucy Lawless in the TV series *Xena – Warrior Princess*. Accordingly, the planet's moon was nicknamed Gabrielle after Xena's travelling companion. The team who discovered the planet claimed they'd 'always wanted to call something Xena' but the name also fitted in with the name Planet X, a name first suggested by Sir William Herschel for the planet he believed existed beyond Uranus. Arguments raged for a while over what it should be called and thousands of Xena fans petitioned the International Astronomical Union. But the IAU was not swayed and Eris it became. However, the IAU may have had the last laugh as Eris is named after the goddess of discord and strife – appropriate for a warrior princess – and the official name of Eris's moon is now Dysnomia . . . which is Greek for 'lawless'. An astronomers' in-joke or just a coincidence?

Lucy Lawless's Xena character first appeared in the TV series *Hercules: The Legendary Journeys* starring Kevin Sorbo as the son of Zeus. Such was the popularity of the character, she spawned her own TV series. Much of both *Hercules* and *Xena* played with aspects of ancient Greek mythology.

The Greeks believed that their Gods lived atop Mount Olympus. Olympus is the highest mountain in Greece, at 9,570 feet. If measured from base to top, it is one of Europe's tallest mountains as its base is at sea level. There is also a Mount Olympus in Cyprus, one in Utah and another in Washington State. But all of these are mole hills compared to the one on Mars.

Olympus Mons (Latin for Mount Olympus) is an

extinct volcano that stands around 17 miles (about 88,600 feet) high above the mean surface level of Mars, making it approximately three times the height of Mount Everest. It is 342 miles across and covers an area the size of Arizona or nearly four times the size of Scotland. The volcano is so massive that it was visible from Earth by nineteenth-century astronomers.

Those same astronomers would have also been able to see the foreskin of Jesus through their telescopes. According to the seventeenth-century theologian Leone Allacci (known by his Latin name Leo Allatius), the rings around Saturn were formed by the divine ascension of the Holy Prepuce.

As a Jew, the infant Jesus would have been circumcised on the eighth day following his birth. In fact the Gospel of Luke actually has the Archangel Gabriel instructing Mary and Joseph to get the deed done in the Temple of Jerusalem. But what happened to the foreskin, or prepuce, afterwards? Putting aside Allatius' somewhat bizarre theory, there have been many claims over the years to possess this most unusual holy relic. During the Middle Ages, the abbey of Charroux in France claimed to have the prepuce after being given it by Charlemagne. It was allegedly taken to Rome in the twelfth century so that Pope Innocent III could vouch for its authenticity but, unsurprisingly perhaps, the Pope elected not to examine the object. For some reason it then went missing and remained lost until 1856, when a workman repairing the abbey claimed to have found it in a reliquary hidden inside a wall. In the meantime other claimants had come forward including the Lateran basilica in Rome, the Cathedral of Le Puy-en-Velay, Santiago de Compostela, the city of Antwerp and churches in Besançon, Metz, Hildesheim, Calcata and the abbey church of Coulombs in Chartres.

However, all modern attempts to discover the whereabouts of the foreskin have failed. The last purported sighting was in 1983, when the people of Calcata in Italy paraded their reliquary through the streets during the Feast of the Circumcision (1 January). The jewel-encrusted box was stolen shortly afterwards and, despite pleas from the Church, has never reappeared. Conspiracy theorists claim that someone, somewhere (everyone from neo-Nazis to aliens have been cited) is growing a clone Jesus from his foreskin. Most well-known was the Second Coming Project, a website set up in 2000 that stated, 'No longer can we rely on hope and prayer, waiting around futilely for Jesus to return. We have the technology to bring him back right now. There is no reason, moral, legal or Biblical, not to take advantage of it. In order to save the world from sin, we must clone Jesus to initiate the second coming of the Christ.' The site asked for donations to this worthy cause. Of course, the whole thing turned out to be a hoax – perpetrated by a chap called Kristan Lawson.

The term clone is derived from the Greek word for twig. Cloning means making an exact genetic copy of an organism. Natural clones exist in the form of identical twins, which are formed from the splitting of a single fertilized egg and are therefore genetically identical. Non-identical twins are formed by two eggs being fertilized simultaneously by two sperm. Non-naturally-occurring clones are created under laboratory conditions by taking existing genetic material from a living creature and using it to grow an identical copy of the donor. To date, the most complex organisms cloned in this way have been a cat, two horses, a mule, a Rhesus monkey and, curiously, a pig called Xena.

The process is far from perfected; the two horses, Prometa and Paris Texas, for example, took 328 and 400+ attempts respectively before a viable embryo was produced.

The first successfully cloned mammal was, of course,

Dolly the sheep, who was cloned from an adult cell at the Roslin Institute in Scotland in 1996 and lived there until her death when she was six. The name Dolly was chosen after a researcher suggested that the sheep be named after Dolly Parton ... because she'd been cloned from a mammary cell.

Dolly Parton is arguably the most successful – and certainly the most buxom – country and western star of all time. She has had 25 songs reach number one on the Billboard country charts, 41 Top Ten country albums and 110 charting singles. She has sold over 100 million records around the world, has received seven Grammy Awards (and 42 nominations) and has won countless country music awards. In addition, she was awarded the Living Legend Medal by the US Library of Congress for her contributions to the cultural heritage of the United States and the National Medal of Arts, the highest honour given by the US government for excellence in the arts. She has received several Golden Globe nominations for her acting and two Academy Award nominations for her songs. There is a bronze sculpture of her on the courthouse lawn in Sevierville, Tennessee (her home town) and she has a star on the Hollywood Walk of Fame, a star on the

Nashville Star Walk for Grammy winners, and a star somewhere barely (if at all) visible in the night sky.

According to the International Star Registry (ISR) there is a star called Dolly Parton; Elvis can be found in the constellation of Cepheus; and more than ten Princess Dianas can be found in the night sky along with Frank Sinatra, Sammy Davis Jr, John F. Kennedy and the cast of *Star Trek*. Or can they?

For a minimum fee of anything between £49.95 and £100, you too could ask the ISR to name a star after you. However, as the International Astronomical Union (IAU) point out, these names have no validity and no astronomer is going to acknowledge them. In fact, the IAU has called the ISR's star-naming business 'a deplorable commercial trick' as you are essentially paying for nothing more than being listed by ISR itself.

The names of astronomical objects are determined solely by the IAU. Star names come to us from folk-lore, mythology and location (such as Polaris). Stars are identified in three ways: by their IAU name, a numerical designation, and a description that relates to their relative brightness. This last name uses letters of the Greek alphabet. Thus Alpha Pegasus is the brightest star in the constellation of Pegasus. Beta Pegasus would be the second brightest ... and so on. After the last (twenty-fourth) letter of the Greek alphabet has been used (for example, Omega Pegasus – if there was one) any remaining stars in the constellation are given a number – for instance, 25 Pegasus.

Names for planets come from Roman mythology as do the names of most moons. Craters and other planetary features are named by various conventions. For example, the names of famous female scientists and philosophers are used for naming features on Venus. The IAU can block what it considers inappropriate names, as it did with Xena and Gabrielle, but usually asteroids and other small bodies are named by their discoverers. Like Eric.

The Asteroid Belt is a huge circle of rocks ...

GOLD, FRANKINCENSE
AND OGRES

The BBC television programme *Torchwood* takes its name from an anagram of 'Doctor Who'. When the BBC decided to resurrect *Doctor Who* in 2005 – after an absence of some 16 years (not counting the TV movie in 1996) – filming was naturally kept top secret to preserve the surprise. As part of the secrecy scripts and other correspondence all bore the code name Torchwood. Later, when the *Doctor Who* series required the creation of a secret government organization dedicated to fighting alien threats, Torchwood was the obvious name to use. The Torchwood Institute has now been given its own spin-off series.

As we saw in Round 6, the Doctor, as he refers to himself, has been played by a number of actors. This is one of the reasons why *Doctor Who* is the longest-running science fiction series in history. The Doctor has the whole of time and space to play with, and the lead and support actors can be changed at any time. It's the ultimate format, allowing for endlessly inventive stories and plotlines. Ten actors have played the Doctor in the BBC series. However, a lot more people have played him outside the 'official' BBC list. Richard Hurndall replaced the late first doctor William Hartnell in the twentieth-anniversary special 'The Five Doctors'. Trevor Martin and David Banks played him in stage shows. On the radio, audiobooks and on the Internet he has been played by Richard E. Grant, Geoffrey Bayldon, David Warner, David Collings, Ian Brooker, Derek Jacobi, Nicholas Briggs, Arabella Weir and Jon Culshaw. In various spoof charity episodes he has been played by Rowan Atkinson, Jim Broadbent, Richard E. Grant, Hugh Grant, Mark Gatiss and Joanna Lumley. A further 40-odd other actors have played the Doctor in fan-produced films and audio adventures. And in the two feature movies made in the 1960s he was played by Peter Cushing.

Peter Cushing (1913–94) had a long and distinguished acting career. In one of his earliest roles he appeared as a student in Laurel and Hardy's *A Chump at Oxford* (1940). However, he is best remembered as one of the stalwarts of the Hammer horror films made during the 1960s and '70s, where he often shared star billing with his good friend Christopher Lee. Together, they appeared in some 22 films with Lee usually playing the monster to Cushing's hero. They also both appeared in George Lucas's epic *Star Wars* saga, although their appearances were some 25 years apart. Cushing appeared as Grand Moff Tarkin in the first film – now *Episode 4: A New Hope* – in 1977 and Lee made his first appearance as Count Dooku in *Episode 2: Attack of the Clones* in 2002. Cushing also apparently reappears as Tarkin at the end of *Episode 3: Revenge of the Sith* (2005). During a scene showing the Death Star being built, Moff Tarkin takes command from Darth Vader. This scene was achieved by using an actor of similar looks and build (Wayne Pygram – best known for playing Scorpius in the series *Farscape*) and CGI using footage of the now deceased Cushing.

'Star Wars' was the nickname of the USA's Strategic Defence Initiative (SDI), first suggested by then-president Ronald Reagan in 1983. He proposed that a shield of ground-, air- and space-based weapons be established over America to protect it from nuclear ballistic missile attack. The more fanciful aspects of the plan suggested orbiting satellites capable of knocking

missiles and planes from the air with laser-type technology. Other components of the programme included
hypervelocity rail guns, particle beams, extended-range
interceptor missiles and a system of satellite-based
rugby-ball-sized mini-missiles called Brilliant Pebbles.

Pebbles Flintstone was born to Fred and Wilma
Flintstone at 8 p.m. on 22 February 10,000 BC. She
was delivered at Rockville Hospital and weighed a
healthy 6 pounds 12 ounces (a little lighter than an
Oscar). In later years, she became an advertising
executive and married the world's strongest boy and
her childhood sweetheart, Bamm-Bamm Rubble, and
took on the hyphenated surname of Flintstone-Rubble.
They produced two children of their own, twin brother
and sister Chip and Roxy. Roxy inherited her father's
great strength. The Flintstone and Rubble families
lived in the fictional town of Bedrock.

Bedrock is the native rock that lies underneath the
soil and other sediments. As such it has come to mean
solidity or firm foundation. Consequently it is a popular name with companies wanting to promote themselves as something substantial or worthy. Bedrock
AM is the hospital radio service offered by Queen's
Hospital, Havering. Havering is one of London's 32
boroughs. Situated within the county of Essex on the

north-east edge of outer London, its principal town is Romford and there are other large residential areas at Hornchurch and Upminster.

The term 'havering' is also a verb and is defined as 'to babble or to talk nonsense' or 'to be slow or hesitant in making a decision'. The word has fallen out of use in common English parlance although it is still used in Scotland. It features in the lyrics of the Proclaimers' 1993 hit 'I'm Gonna Be (500 Miles)':

> *If I haver . . . yeah I know I'm gonna be*
> *I'm gonna be the man who's havering to you.*

The Proclaimers are identical twins Charlie and Craig Reid. Their political soulful acoustic songs have only occasionally made it into the singles charts but their albums have always sold well. Their songs are also frequently used in movie soundtracks and have appeared in (among others) *Benny and Joon*, *Dumb and Dumber* and *Shrek*.

Shrek! was originally a children's book written and illustrated by prolific cartoonist William Steig (1907–2003). The name is taken from the German and Yiddish word *shreck*, which means fear or terror.

During a lengthy career Steig drew cartoons for

many books and magazines including over 117 covers for the *New Yorker* magazine. At the age of 61, when most people are contemplating retirement, he reinvented himself as a children's book author. His rapier wit and sense of irony transferred from his cartoons into his children's books, which are famously crude and witty in much the same way that Roald Dahl's works are. Steig can also lay claim to inventing the contemporary greetings card. As he once pointed out during an interview for the *Hartford Courant*, 'Greeting cards used to be all sweetness and love. I started doing the complete reverse – almost a hate card – and it caught on.' Steig's cards featured satirical cartoons and savage caricatures of people like kleptomaniacs, alcoholics, amnesiacs and characters with emotional problems.

The greetings cards industry is huge, worth an estimated £1.2 billion in the UK and over $7 billion in the USA. And that's annually. There are many companies producing cards but the industry is dominated by giants such as Clinton and Hallmark.

Hallmark is truly a mega-company with outlets in over 100 countries and employing 21,000 staff. Its profits are equally massive. However, many consider it a model company as it gives 5 per cent of its profits to charitable causes and has had an employee profit-sharing scheme since 1956. It has also been applauded for actively supporting working women. In recent years the Hallmark name and crown logo have also been used for family TV channels such as the eponymous Hallmark Channel, which is owned by Crown Media Holdings Inc.

The crown, of course, is a symbolic form of head-gear usually worn by a monarch. The word comes from 'corona,' which means wreath. Crowns originate from the tradition of rewarding triumphant generals, monarchs and athletes with a small wreath of leaves that was worn on the head. To this day, high-ranking police and military officers still wear badges of rank that incorporate laurel or bay leaf wreath designs. Jesus was mocked by the Romans as 'King of the Jews' by the placing of a wreath or crown of thorns on his head during his execution.

When Jesus was first born, he was visited by three crown wearers – the three kings or Magi. *Magi* is the Latinized plural of the Greek word *magos*, which referred specifically to a priestly caste of Zoroastrians who were expert astrologers. This area of what was then seen as science gave birth to modern astronomy and mathematics. Consequently, the Magi are also frequently referred to as the Wise Men.

The Magi brought three symbolic gifts for the infant Jesus: gold, frankincense and myrrh. It has been suggested that the gold was in a medicinal form as frankincense and myrrh also had mystic and medicinal uses.

Frankincense and myrrh are obtained from trees of the *Burseraceae* family, which is found in tropical regions of the Americas, Africa and Asia. These 40-odd species also produce the resin called copal and burn well due to the high resin content of their wood. Consequently, the common name for this family of trees is Torchwoods.

The BBC television programme *Torchwood* takes its name from . . .

GHOST SHIPS, AMAZONS AND MURRAY MINTS

To give chickens CPR you need to pump their legs up and down. CPR stands for Cardiopulmonary resuscitation and refers to an emergency first aid procedure used on a person who has suffered cardiac arrest.

Cardiac Arrest is the title of a 1980 film starring Fred Ward and Gary Goodrow. The plot involves a serial killer who removes the hearts of his victims. The investigation (by a weak-stomached homicide cop) discovers a black market for human organs. Meanwhile, a man must make a difficult decision regarding his wife, who needs a transplant. Should he try to contact the killer to buy a heart? The film was written and directed by one Mr Murray Mintz.

Murray Mints are an old-fashioned, buttery and mildly minty lozenge produced in the UK by the

Cadbury Trebor Bassett sweet company. No one seems to know who Murray was as the origins of the sweet have been lost in a long series of company mergers and acquisitions. What we do know is that they first appeared in 1944 and were the very first product in history to have an advertising jingle written for them. The commercial featured animated guardsmen marching to the strains of

> *Murray Mints! Murray Mints!*
> *Too good to hurry mints!*

The jingle was recorded by Cliff Adams and the Stargazers, who famously performed it live during a broadcast of *Sunday Night at the London Palladium*. They finished by throwing Murray Mints to the audience. The Stargazers began their career as backing singers for UK singer Petula Clark.

The term stargazer usually denotes an astronomer, someone who studies the various physical features that exist beyond the Earth. However, it can also be used to describe an astrologer, who reads meaning into the movement of the stars and other celestial bodies. The disciplines have a common origin as early stargazing encompassed elements of both astronomy and astrology.

Modern scientific astronomy received a hefty boost when telescopes became widely available. Galileo Galilei (1564–1642) is often credited with the invention of the telescope but he merely perfected existing devices built by three Dutchmen, Hans Lippershey and Zacharias Janssen (spectacle makers from Middelburg) and Jacob Metius of Alkmaar. Long before this, people were using lenses of varying quality to observe distant objects. There is also some evidence of early telescope development in the writings of eleventh-century Iraqi astronomer Ibn al-Haytham.

Galileo was born in Pisa, and although he never married and was a devout Roman Catholic, sired three children with a lady called Marina Gamba. The children were named Virginia, Livia and Vincenzio. Because they were born out of wedlock, the two girls entered a convent where they stayed for the rest of their lives. Livia took the name of Sister Arcangela while Virginia became known as Sister Maria Celeste. She chose her name in honour of the Virgin Mary and her father's love of astronomy. In recent years an impact crater on Venus was named after her. The anglicized version of her name is Mary Celeste.

The *Mary Celeste* was a ship that has become the centre of one of the world's most enduring mysteries.

The legend goes that on the morning of Friday 13 December 1872 a small two-masted ship was seen entering the Bay of Gibraltar. When the vessel was boarded, it was found that the *Mary Celeste* was entirely abandoned: there was no trace of Captain Benjamin Briggs, his wife and child, nor the seven crew. The American ship showed signs of a speedy abandonment – food was left half-eaten on the tables, a cup of oil sat next to a sewing machine – and there were curious traces of what looked like blood on a handrail and on a sword under the captain's bed. The cargo of alcohol was still intact in the hold and the boarders became aware of an eerie, spooky atmosphere . . .

Hundreds of theories have since been put forward to explain the mystery including a curse (Friday the thirteenth), sea monsters, madness caused by gas, mutineers, pirates and abduction by aliens. However the truth may be rather more mundane.

Much of the version we know today comes from a short story written by the young Arthur Conan Doyle – later to write the Sherlock Holmes stories. In his 1884 tale *The Captain of the Polestar* Conan Doyle took the real story of the *Mary Celeste* and 'sexed it up' for publication. He changed the name of the ship to *Marie Celeste* and invented a whole range of mysterious features to make the mystery even spookier. Not surprisingly, Conan Doyle's story caught the public imagination and his version of events is often mistaken for the true story.

The known facts are that the ship was boarded on 4 December, not the thirteenth. The ship did look as if it had been abandoned but most of the features mentioned by Conan Doyle were not present. The so-called blood was rust. A lifeboat was missing but was never found. However, in early 1873 five (some accounts say six) highly decomposed bodies were found tied to two rafts (or two lifeboats) off the coast of Spain. One was flying an American flag. This could be the ultimate fate of the crew but no formal identification was ever made. The *Mary Celeste* herself went on for another 12 years before she was grounded during a failed insurance scam in Haiti.

So what really happened? We may never know, but the most popular current theory relates to a seaquake. American researcher Captain David Williams[22], has

---

22 http://www.deafwhale.com/maryceleste/

established that on 5 November 1872 the seismological station in Zurich recorded a large earthquake with its epicentre in the Atlantic Ocean exactly where the *Mary Celeste* would have been at the time. It may be that Captain Briggs felt the quake and believed his ship to be sinking, as the vibrations would have caused damage consistent with the actual damage found, such as the stove breaking free. Consequently the crew may have abandoned ship in good faith but – for reasons unknown – did not survive the experience.

Whatever the truth, the ship had a career dogged by bad luck, both before and after Briggs was captain. Some superstitious people point out that this may be due to the fact that its name was changed – apparently something you should never do to a ship. The *Mary Celeste*'s original name was the *Amazon*.

The Amazons were a nation of female warriors in Greek mythology. The Greek historian Herodotus stated that they were descendants of the nomadic Sarmatian people who eventually settled in south-east Europe. He also reported some unusual customs including men and women wearing the same clothes, and women not marrying until they had killed a man in battle. Most extraordinary was that the women had no right breasts. Hippocrates described a painful-sounding procedure whereby a red-hot bronze instrument was used on infant girls to cauterize the tissue so that the breast never developed. Thus, in his words, 'all its strength and bulk are diverted to the right shoulder and right arm'. The lack of a breast also allowed longer pulls on a bowstring.

The Amazon river in South America is, in a roundabout way, named after these legendary warrior women. The conquistador Francisco de Orellana fought a battle with the Tapuyas tribe while exploring the river. The Tapuyas women were reported to fight alongside their men with equal strength and savagery, although some historians believe that what Orellana took to be women were actually long-haired Amerindian warriors. In due course, and recalling the fighting women of Greek myth, Orellana named the river Rio Amazonas in their honour.

The Amazon winds its way through the lushest rainforest in the world. It is a region where there is a greater diversity of life than anywhere else on the planet. Yet, until recently, there was little evidence of prehistoric life in the region. The fossil record is almost non-existent because the high humidity causes relatively rapid decay of tissues and bones. However, in 2003 fossil remains were found of a diplodocus-like sauropod, which was named *Amazonsaurus maranhensis*. It was about 30 feet long and weighed approximately ten tons, making it one of the smallest sauropods ever discovered. Amazonsaurus is the first dinosaur to be found in the Amazon Basin, although if you accept the theory that birds are the modern descendants of dinosaurs, the area is particularly rich in varieties and species.

There now seems to be overwhelming evidence of the dinosaur–bird transition with many feathered dinosaur fossils being found along with those of primitive toothed birds. This evidence has been further bolstered by the recent discovery of a naturally occurring mutant chicken called a talpid, which has a complete set of crocodile-like teeth. The discoverers, a scientific team based at the Universities of Manchester, UK and Wisconsin, USA, have also managed to induce teeth growth in normal chickens, activating genes that have lain dormant for 80 million years.

To give chickens CPR, you need to pump their legs up and down . . .

YES, PORN HAD TO BE MENTIONED EVENTUALLY . . .

Kylie Minogue turned down the offer of singing a duet with James Dean Bradfield on the Manic Street Preachers 1992 album *Generation Terrorists*. Instead, the vocals on the track 'Little Baby Nothing' – a song about the sexual exploitation of women – were sung by ex-porn star Traci Lords.

Traci Lords is now a respectable mainstream actress but she was not always so. Born Nora Louise Kuzma on 7 May 1968, she achieved notoriety by appearing in pornographic films and *Penthouse* magazine when she was just 15 years old. By the time she was 18, she'd appeared in over 100 adult films, all of which are considered illegal in the USA where porn stars have to be over 18. Many of the films' directors, producers, technicians and stars were prosecuted but Lords herself was never charged with a crime, as she was a minor. The films were, and still are, banned in the United States . . . all except one: *Traci, I Love You* was made after Lords' eighteenth birthday and the rights are solely owned by her. This is the only film from which she was ever able to draw a decent income, which has led to unsubstantiated claims that it was Lords herself who tipped off the authorities about her underage activities.

Traci Lords took her stage name from a school-friend and from Jack Lord, star of the long-running series *Hawaii Five-O*, who was her favourite actor as a child. The *Five-O* refers to the fact that Hawaii became America's fiftieth state in 1959.

The Hawaiian Islands were known as the Sandwich Islands for many years and still appear as such on some maps. They were named in 1778 by Captain James Cook in honour of the First Lord of the Admiralty, John Montagu, 4th Earl of Sandwich. This is the same Lord Sandwich after whom the popular snack is named. Legend has it that he was so busy working at his desk that he didn't have time to eat. When he was implored to take some food by his staff, he asked that a slice of good beef be brought to him between two pieces of bread. Another story is that this particular form of snack was invented as a way for him to remain at the gaming tables. Following his stint at the Admiralty in 1753, he became one of the principal secretaries of state and was one of the people responsible for prosecuting John Wilkes for libel.

Wilkes (1725–97) – once described as 'the ugliest man in England' – was a notorious rake with a curiously protruding jaw and a squint. Despite this, he was popular with both ladies and men because of his rapier wit. For example, when Sandwich remarked, 'Wilkes, I don't know whether you'll die upon the gallows or of the pox,' he quickly replied, 'That depends, my Lord, whether I first embrace your Lordship's principles, or your Lordship's mistresses.' His career was one of extraordinary highs and lows. He became MP for Aylesbury, Buckinghamshire in 1757 and launched frequent and verbal attacks on the prime minister, the Earl of Bute, mainly because it was well known that George III had arranged Bute's appointment and he was clearly incompetent. Wilkes then started a newspaper called *The North Briton* and used it to attack Bute and other senior politicians. However, this led to him first being challenged and wounded in a duel by Samuel Martin and then being charged with seditious libel and expelled from the House of Commons. Before he could be arrested, his friends arranged for him to be whisked away to Paris. But you can't keep a good man down and, when his money ran out, Wilkes returned to the UK expecting to be arrested – but, to his surprise, wasn't.

Wilkes being Wilkes, he once again entered the political arena and got himself elected MP for Middlesex. This was followed (unsurprisingly) by his immediate arrest and imprisonment for previous offences. He was sentenced to 22 months imprisonment and a £1000 fine. But there was civil unrest at his arrest, and for two weeks a large crowd of protesters gathered near the prison at St George's Fields shouting for Wilkes' release and chanting anti-royal slogans. The mob reached in excess of 15,000 and so scared the prison authorities that they opened fire, killing seven protesters.

Wilkes was elected MP for Middlesex three times during his incarceration (February, March and April, 1769) but the election result was overturned each time by Parliament. This led to the formation of the Bill of Rights Society to demand that Parliament accept the will of the people. When Wilkes was released in 1770 he was still banned from political office so he became a champion of free speech. Subsequently, he was elected a sheriff in London and then Lord Mayor in 1774. In the same year he once again regained the seat for Middlesex and spent his remaining years in the Commons campaigning for parliamentary reform.

Wilkes and Sandwich were both members of the Hellfire Club, also known as the Knights of St Francis of Wycombe, or the Medmenham Monks.

The Hellfire Club was the popular name for an exclusive English society that met irregularly from 1746 to around 1763 at the Dashwood Estate in West Wycombe, Buckinghamshire. The club, run by Sir Francis Dashwood (known as the Abbot) took part in pseudo-religious and mock-satanic rituals but its main purpose was the consumption of food, drink, drugs and sex. Early meetings took place at the nearby restored Medmenham Abbey, but then Dashwood decided to create a dedicated venue and extended a series of prehistoric caves carved into the chalk hill above his estate.

The initial membership of the club was limited to 12 but it soon increased. Among its more notorious members were the aforementioned John Wilkes and the 4th Earl of Sandwich, the Earl of Bute (the prime minister), William Hogarth, the Marquis of Granby, the Prince of Wales and Horace Walpole. Benjamin Franklin occasionally attended the club's meetings but wasn't a full 'Brother'. Female guests were called Nuns, all the more ironic when you consider that the majority were 'dollymops' – prostitutes. The club motto was *Fay ce que vouldras* (Do what thou wilt).[23]

It was a practical joke instigated by Wilkes that may well have been responsible for the club's dissolution. Wilkes smuggled a live baboon into the caves and hid it in a box. When the evening's ceremony kicked off, Wilkes tugged on a thin cord, and the latch opened. The baboon leapt out and Sandwich, believing it to be the Devil himself, is reported to have cried out in panic, 'Spare me, gracious Devil! Spare a wretch who never was sincerely your servant! I sinned only from vanity of being in the fashion; thou knowest I never have been half so wicked as I pretended: never have been able to commit the thousandth part of the vices

---

23 From François Rabelais and later used as a motto by magician and all-round odd bloke Aleister Crowley.

which I have boasted of . . . Leave me therefore and go to those who are more truly devoted to your service. I am but half a sinner!'

No wonder Sandwich was happy to aid in Wilkes' prosecution. The event so rattled the Brothers that membership of the Hellfire Club slowly but surely dwindled and died.

Baboons (*Papio ursinus*) are one of the largest members of the monkey family. Some adult males can weigh as much as 88 pounds. They are predominantly ground-dwellers and walk on four powerful limbs. They live in well-organized male-dominated troops or, as some would have it, flanges.

The term flange has become more popular in recent years as the collective noun for baboons. It even features in the official list published by the Oxford English Dictionary (which also includes such delights as a bike of ants, a shrewdness of apes, a destruction of cats, a drift of quail, an escargatoire of snails and a knob of widgeon) yet its origin can be traced back to a sketch from the BBC satirical comedy show *Not the Nine O'Clock News*. The sketch, first shown in 1979, featured a talking gorilla called Gerald, who explained that the collective noun for gorillas is a whoop and for baboons a flange. Both terms were entirely made up by the writers but have now entered general usage.

The cast of *Not the Nine O'Clock News* went on to become successful solo artists. Pamela Stephenson appeared in several films and TV series before becoming a psychologist and writer – most famously penning the best-selling official biography of her husband, comedian Billy Connolly. Mel Smith and Griff Rhys Jones established a double act and appeared in several TV series of *Alas Smith and Jones* and feature films including *Morons from Outer Space* and *Wilt*. Rhys Jones is now a TV presenter and writer, and Smith a film director. Most successful of all was Rowan Atkinson, who scored huge successes with the *Blackadder* and *Mr Bean* TV series. Mr Bean has also made it to the big screen in two movies and Atkinson has appeared in many other films. They include *Never Say Never Again*, *Keeping Mum*, *Love Actually*, *Four Weddings and a Funeral* and *The Lion King*. He took the lead role in spy spoof *Johnny English* opposite Australian actress and singer Natalie Imbruglia.

Natalie Imbruglia is one of several Australian actors and actresses who have found worldwide fame after first appearing in the Australian soap opera *Neighbours*. Others who have benefited from appearances on the show are Russell Crowe, Jason Donovan, Alan Dale, Peter Andre, Guy Pearce, Holly Valance and, most successfully of all, Kylie Minogue.

Kylie Minogue turned down the offer of singing a duet with . . .

Round 25

CATS . . . PROBABLY

The expression 'to let the cat out of the bag' has its origin in a marketplace scam from the seventeenth century. The scam was aimed at those looking to purchase a suckling pig – a small sweet-tasting piglet still taking milk from its mother. Dishonest vendors would offer a piglet for sale but then substitute a cat for the piglet and hand it over in a sealed bag. Only when the unfortunate buyer let the cat out of the bag would they discover the truth.

Interestingly, this also gives us the expression 'a pig in a poke' as poke is a corruption of *poche* meaning bag . . . which is where we also get the word pocket from. And poacher too, as poachers often had special pockets sewn into their clothing to hide their illegal kills.[24] Incidentally, the term poach when used in

_____

24 Another theory traces 'poacher' back to the obsolete French word *pocher*, meaning to intrude, thrust or trespass.

cooking also derives from the term for bag because of the physical appearance of poached eggs.

The most famous poacher of all time is undoubtedly Robin Hood, who is supposed to have hidden with his gang among the trees of Sherwood Forest, living upon the king's poached deer and boars, and gifts of food from peasants they had helped. There are many candidates for the historical Robin Hood, including Robert Fitzodo, Robert of Loxley, Robert de Kyme and a certain Robert Hod, but we will probably never know who he was, if indeed he ever existed. The name may be a corruption of robehod, hobbehod or rabunhod, a general term for robber or villain that appears in county rolls all over the country from the eleventh century onwards. The term was still in use in 1605 when Robert Cecil described Guy Fawkes and his not-so-merry men as Robin Hoods. The first quasi-historical reference to the character we know today was when Andrew of Wyntoun mentions in his *Orygynal Chronicle* (*c.*1420) that 'Robyne Hude' was plying his trade around 1293.

However, none of this has stopped Hollywood or TV companies making a fortune from the character. The BBC recently ran a new version of the story as a successful drama series, and back in the 1980s ITV ran a popular series called *Robin of Sherwood* in which Robin was played first by Michael Praed and then by Jason Connery, son of James Bond star Sean. The series was notable for its haunting music, written and performed by Irish band Clannad, and for helping to launch the careers of a number of fine British actors including Ray Winstone (Will Scarlet) and Clive Mantle (Little John).

Clive Mantle has gone on to appear in many television shows, films and theatre productions. At six feet five and a half inches tall, he is an imposing figure and his height was used to great comic effect in *The Vicar of Dibley* when, as Simon Horton, he briefly became the love interest of five-foot-tall Geraldine Grainger (Dawn French).

The Vicar of Dibley is one of the UK's most popular sitcoms and charts the adventures and misadventures of a female vicar among the eccentric denizens of a small Oxfordshire village. Although now accepted by most people, women priests were still very new when the series began and the creators received hate mail from angry Anglicans. The man behind the series was comedy writer Richard Curtis, who also wrote the screenplays to a host of successful movies including *Love Actually*, *Four Weddings and a Funeral*, *The Tall*

Guy, *Bridget Jones* (1 and 2) and *Notting Hill*. He was also the co-creator of *Blackadder* and a writer on the *Spitting Image*, *Mr Bean* and *Not the Nine O'Clock News* TV series.

Not the Nine O'Clock News was one of the finest comedy shows ever put out by the BBC and part of the reason for this was its open door policy regarding material. Although the programme was built around a core of in-house writers, the producers were willing to look at any submissions they were sent. If it was funny enough, the sketch went in. Many famous names appear on its list of guest writers including Stephen Fry, John Lloyd, Clive Anderson, Ruby Wax, Rory McGrath, Nigel Planer and Douglas Adams.

Adams, of course, was the best-selling author of the *Hitchhiker's Guide to the Galaxy* in all of its various and contradictory forms. Starting on radio, it then became a novel, a stage play, a computer game, a TV series and ultimately (sadly after Adams's untimely death) a major Hollywood movie. All of these had slightly different plots, timelines and characters as if Adams could never quite decide the version he liked best. Adams also wrote two books with another set of characters: *Dirk Gently's Holistic Detective Agency* and its sequel, *The Long Dark Tea-Time of the Soul*.

In both series of books Adams discusses the subject of probability. In the Hitchhiker series, the starship *Heart of Gold* is powered by the Infinite Improbability Drive, which works on the absurd principle that infinite amounts of improbability are generated allowing the ship to pass through almost every point in the universe simultaneously. Therefore, it's just a simple matter of knowing when to stop. Meanwhile, in the Dirk Gently books, a disappearing cat, a ghost and a curious murder lead Dirk to ponder upon the nature of probability. And to explain it, he uses the story of Schrödinger's cat.

Schrödinger's cat is a thought experiment designed by physicist Erwin Schrödinger to demonstrate probability. As Adams explains it in *Dirk Gently's Holistic Detective Agency*:

So you imagine that you take a cat and put it in a box that you can seal completely. Also in the box you put a small lump of radioactive material, and a phial of poison gas. You arrange it so that within a given period of time there is an exactly fifty-fifty chance that an atom in the radioactive lump will decay and emit an electron. If it does decay then it triggers the release of the gas and kills the cat. If it doesn't, the cat lives. Fifty-fifty. Depending on the fifty-fifty chance that a single atom does or does not decay. The point as I understand it is this: since the decay of a single atom is a quantum level event that wouldn't be resolved either way until it was observed, and since you don't make the observation until you open the box and see whether the cat is alive or dead, then there's a rather extraordinary consequence. Until you do open the box the cat itself exists in an indeterminate state. The possibility that it is alive, and the possibility that it is dead, are two different waveforms superimposed on each other inside the box.[25]

In other words, two different probabilities exist and it is only when the box is opened that the truth is revealed and probability becomes certainty. Letting the cat out of the box curiously parallels letting the cat out of the bag as both reveal the truth.

The expression 'to let the cat out of the bag' has its origin in a marketplace scam . . .

---

25 Another rather more silly thought experiment involving cats and probability was created by US comedian Steven Wright. It goes like this . . . we all know that toast always lands butter side down. And that cats always land on their feet. So what would happen if we strapped a piece of toast butter side up to a cat's back and threw it off the roof? Would it just hover?

Aloha Buck

In 2001 UK rock band Feeder recorded a song called 'Buck Rogers', one of their biggest hits to date.

Buck Rogers started life as a character called Anthony Rogers in two novellas called 'Armageddon 2419 AD' and 'The Airlords of Han' written by Philip Francis Nowlan. They appeared in the pulp magazine *Amazing Stories* in 1928 and 1929. The stories caught the imagination of John F. Dille, president of the National Newspaper Service syndicate, who asked if the character could be turned into a comic strip. He also suggested the name Buck in reference to popular cowboy stories and films from the 1920s featuring Buck Jones. Thus, *Buck Rogers in the 25th Century* was born, written by Nowlan and illustrated by Dick Calkins. It was the first ever science fiction cartoon strip and an immediate success. It is said that its popularity helped open the minds of many Americans to the idea of space travel.

In time, it became a radio show (1932–47) and a successful movie serial starring ex-Olympic gold medallist swimmer-turned-actor Larry 'Buster' Crabbe (1939). Later, it became a TV series (1950–51) and ultimately a big-budget TV movie and two series (1979–81) starring Gil Gerard. There have also been many novels, computer games, role-playing games and short stories based on the character. And Warner Brothers famously spoofed the series in one of their most popular Daffy Duck *Looney Tunes* ever, *Duck Dodgers in the 24½th Century* (1953).

The 1979–81 series were made by prolific TV producer Glen A. Larson, who also produced such iconic cult series as *Battlestar Galactica*, *Alias Smith and Jones*, *Knight Rider*, *The Fall Guy*, *Manimal*, *Automan* and *The Six Million Dollar Man*. *The Six Million Dollar Man* starred Lee Majors as robotically enhanced astronaut Steve Austin who, thanks to his new bionic parts, could run at amazing speeds, see astounding distances and bash his way through steel plating. The series was developed from a novel by author Martin Caidin (1927–97) called *Cyborg* (1972). Curiously, Caidin also wrote a Buck Rogers novel,

Buck Rogers: A Life in the Future (1995), in which he reinvented the character for a modern audience. Having been cryogenically suspended for 500 years after a horrific plane crash, Rogers is defrosted and repaired using Caidin's beloved bionics.

Glen A. Larson also collaborated with Donald Bellisario to create *Magnum P.I.* starring Tom Selleck (who incidentally was George Lucas's original choice to play Indiana Jones; his *Magnum P.I.* contract prevented it). Apparently, the series was developed solely because the production company had lots of leftover resources in Hawaii following the cancellation of *Hawaii Five-O.*

The star of the *Hawaii Five-O* series was Jack Lord (1920–98), real name John Joseph Patrick Ryan. Actors changing their names is nothing new, of course. We all know that John Wayne's real name was Marion Morrison and that Marilyn Monroe was Norma Jean Baker. But did you know that Michael Crawford is actually Michael Dumble-Smith? Or that Tom Cruise was christened Thomas Cruise Mapother IV? James Garner's real name is James Bumgarner, and Demi Moore's is Demetria Guynes. Courtney Love once went by the name of Michelle Harrison and Tammy Wynette was once Wynette Pugh. Buck Rogers actor

Larry 'Buster' Crabbe's real name was Clarence Linden Crabbe. And have you ever wondered why Mr. T of *A-Team* fame was so named? It's because his name is Lawrence Tero.

The A-Team featured Mr. T, George Peppard, Dwight Schultz and Dirk Benedict as the heroes. Benedict is seen in the opening credits looking worriedly at a Cylon Centurion, a nod to the fact that he previously played Starbuck in the Glen A. Larson-produced *Battlestar Galactica*, in which the human race was threatened by the robotic Cylons. The character of Mad Murdock (Schultz) often wore T-shirts in the show that gave a clue as to the show's standing. At the end of series four (when there was some indication that series five might not happen) his T-shirt read 'All good things must come to an end'. And in the penultimate and last episodes of the final series the shirts said 'Almost fini' and 'Fini'. The role of Hannibal Smith in *The A-Team* was first offered to James Coburn before being awarded to *Breakfast at Tiffany's* star George Peppard.

As mentioned in a previous Round, *Breakfast at Tiffany's* (1961) also starred Audrey Hepburn, and it is considered by many to be her finest performance. However, her portrayal of Eliza Doolittle in *My Fair*

Lady (1964) runs it close. In this film, based on the George Bernard Shaw play *Pygmalion*, the working-class Doolittle is taught how to pass herself off as a lady by Professor Henry Higgins (Rex Harrison) and the kindly Colonel Pickering, played by Wilfred Hyde White. Harrison also played a character called Dolittle (albeit spelled differently) in the 1957 musical *Dr Dolittle*. Meanwhile, Wilfrid Hyde White went on to appear in both *Battlestar Galactica* and *Buck Rogers in the 25th Century*.

In the 1979 *Buck Rogers* series one episode 'Planet of the Slave Girls' there is a guest appearance by 72-year-old Larry 'Buster' Crabbe as a retired starship pilot called Brigadier Gordon. This is a reference to the fact that Crabbe also portrayed that other great space hero Flash Gordon during the 1930s. This was undoubtedly his most famous role although he did also play Tarzan. This makes him the only actor to have played all three of the most popular pulp heroes of that era – Tarzan, Flash Gordon and Buck Rogers.

In 2001 UK rock band Feeder recorded a song called . . .

UNDER THE SEA . . . UP IN THE AIR . . . SWEET!

Starfish exhibit bizarre anatomical differences from us mammals. They consist of a central disc from which arms sprout in radial symmetry. Most starfish have five arms, but they can have as many as 40 and some have such truncated arms that they look pentagonal in shape. The mouth can be found at the centre of the underside of the animal and is part of an extraordinary eating mechanism. The starfish actually extrudes its own stomach from its mouth and pushes it inside the shell of its snail prey where it then digests the creature's soft tissues. The animal's anus is directly opposite its mouth on the upper, or aboral, surface, which is covered in spines for protection. There is a simple eye on the end of each arm which is sensitive only to light and dark and movement.

Starfish belong to the animal class *Asteroidea*, meaning star-like. *Aster* means star, which is where aster flowers get their name. And astronomy and astrology. And disaster, which means bad star and was once used as a name for comets, which were seen as portents of doom.

Starfish have no brains and no blood. Their nervous system is spread throughout their arms and their vital fluid is actually filtered seawater. A structure on the aboral surface called the madreporite works as a water filter and supplies the starfish's water vascular system. This system allows water to be pumped in and out of the starfish's hundreds of boneless tubular feet, providing motion and grip on prey. But perhaps the most extraordinary aspect of their anatomy is their ability to regenerate new tissue. Almost all starfish can regrow severed arms. And some species can regenerate a whole new body if part of the central ring of nerve tissue is attached. Starfish reproduce by the release of sperm and eggs into the water. Most species produce free-swimming larvae that are bilaterally symmetrical like us. However, they later develop radial symmetry and settle down to life on the seabed.

Starfish are echinoderms – spiny-skinned animals – and their closest relatives are brittle stars, sea urchins, feather stars and holothurians. Holothurians are also known as sea cucumbers due to their shape and are not radially symmetrical. They also differ from other echinoderms in that many species are hermaphrodites, meaning that they have both male and female sex organs and can reproduce both sexually and asexually.

The term hermaphrodite derives from Hermaphroditus, the son of Hermes and Aphrodite in Greek mythology. He became fused with a female nymph and from that point on possessed both male and female sexuality. In medicine the term is considered archaic and has been replaced by intersexual. But some believe that this too is antiquated and the preferred term is now DSD (disorder of sex development). 'The third sex' is also sometimes used but as this can also be used to describe transgendered people, transvestites and even gay people, it is not a precise description.

At a time when homosexuality could be punished with death by hanging, life was difficult for the eighteenth-century third-sex English. But they did manage to meet up at an early form of gay bar. Nicknamed molly houses, premises existed for gay or transgender men to find each other. The most famous molly house was Mother Clap's in Holborn, London, where the patrons (who were called mollies) often dressed in female attire and acted like women. And, who knows? It may have fooled some of the people out to catch them.

Mollies, guppies, platys, swordtails and four-eyed fish (anableps) are closely related species of live-bearing fish. They are hardy and popular aquarium fish and breed well in captivity. Of them all, the guppy (*Poecilia reticulata*) is the best known and most colourful. It's true to say that although many guppies are similar in colour and pattern, no two are ever identical. All live-bearers prefer very lightly salted water as in the wild they live in mildly brackish water and can survive short periods in saltwater conditions.

The guppy is named after Robert John Lechmere Guppy (1836–1916), who discovered the species in Trinidad in 1866. He was known as the Reverend Guppy as he habitually wore what looked like a clergyman's dog collar ... but he was no such thing. He took to wearing the unusual plain white collar as he hated tying neckties.

The Super Guppy is a huge wide-bodied cargo aircraft produced by Aero Spacelines, Inc. used to ferry outsized cargo. It was adapted from the military version of the Boeing 377. It is 141 feet long and has an enormous bulbous cargo area with a diameter of 25 feet and a length of 94 feet 6 inches. It can carry a load of 40,000 pounds and cruise at 300 mph. It looks quite like the fish as pregnant guppies have large swollen bellies.

The Super Guppy has now been superseded by the Airbus A300–600ST Super Transporter or 'Beluga'. It earned its nickname because of its shape, which resembles that of the beluga white whale.[26]

The beluga whale (*Delphinapterus leucas*) lives inside and around the Arctic Circle. 'Beluga' comes from the Russian word for white. It is a close relative of the curious-looking narwhal, which means 'corpse whale' in old Norse, a reference to the animal's mottled white and grey colour. However, the most conspicuous feature of the narwhal is its tusk or tusks, which can grow up to nearly 10 feet long (compared with a body length 13–16 feet) and weigh up to 22 pounds each. Scientists believe that the tusks are used for showmanship and for dominance, but there is some evidence that they

---

26 There is another animal called a beluga. The beluga sturgeon (*Huso huso*) lives in the Caspian and Black Seas, and is one of the world's largest freshwater fish. Unconfirmed reports suggest that belugas may reach a length of up to 28 feet. However, because it can move between seawater and freshwater it is not counted as a true freshwater fish so the 'largest' title goes to the Mekong giant catfish. Beluga are heavily fished for their eggs – beluga caviar.

may be sensory organs as each tusk has millions of tiny tubes within it that connect to the nervous system. These sensors, if that's what they are, could detect temperature, pressure or a host of other environmental factors. Some medieval Europeans believed narwhal tusks to be the horns of the legendary unicorn and they were favourite items for display in a showman's cabinet of curiosities.

Other common cabinet items included Feejee Mermaids. These looked like the small mummified bodies of something part mammal and part fish. Showman Phineas T. Barnum popularized the phenomenon as did Robert Ripley of 'Believe It or Not' fame. Barnum claimed that his Feejee Mermaid had been caught in 1842 by a Dr J. Griffin, but it was in fact (as many were) made by Indonesian craftsmen using papier mâché, pieces of dried fish and stuffed monkeys stitched together.

Unicorns and mermaids are forms of chimera – creatures combining features of different animal species. Mythology is full of them: the gryphon or griffin, for example, was half eagle and half lion (and the surname of Barnum's fake fisherman). Griffin is also the surname of the dysfunctional stars of Fox TV cartoon series *Family Guy*.

Family Guy is set in the fictitious Rhode Island town of Quahog (pronounced 'Coe-hog'). A Quahog is a clam, hence the various references to clams throughout the series, such as the Drunken Clam, Peter Griffin's favourite bar.

Clams are shelled marine or freshwater molluscs belonging to the class *Bivalvia* and are a favourite food, along with mussels, of echinoderms such as sea urchins, sea cucumbers, sand dollars and starfish.

Starfish exhibit bizarre anatomical differences . . .

PARADISE? IT WAS ALL YELLOW

UK band Coldplay took their name from a collection of poems by Philip Horky. The name was suggested by a friend called Tim Rice-Oxley, who was offered a job as Coldplay's keyboard player. He turned the offer down as he was already committed to the band Keane. Keane, who had been called The Lotus Eaters, took their name from Cherry Keane, a friend of lead singer Tom Chaplin's mother. Coldplay were originally called Starfish. Lead singer Chris Martin married actress Gwyneth Paltrow in 2003 and they have two children, Apple and Moses.

The front cover of Coldplay's 2005 *X&Y* album displays an odd arrangement of coloured blocks against a black background. The blocks do, in fact, spell 'X&Y' using the obscure telegrapher's Baudot code.

The code was invented in 1874 by Emile Baudot and uses visual representations of 1s and 0s in a five-digit sequence to indicate the letters of the alphabet and related symbols. It was the first truly digital form of communication and was used for wireless telegraphy until replaced by Morse code.

Morse code was cleverly incorporated into the theme music of the UK TV series *Inspector Morse*. Australian composer Barrington Pheloung spelled out Morse (-- --- ·-· ··· ·) as a recurring musical pattern (a ruder Morse code message was embedded in music by Mike Oldfield, you may recall). *Inspector Morse* was a popular detective series starring the late John Thaw and is notable for the intellectual way Morse and his assistant Lewis decode and solve crimes. Morse is also somewhat of an anti-hero being gruff, pedantic and occasionally misogynistic. A long-kept secret in the series was Morse's first name. It was eventually revealed as Endeavour, as Morse's father had been inspired by the voyages of Captain James Cook and had chosen to name his son after Cook's ship. The series was set in and around the city of Oxford.

An entirely different city of Oxford was used as the setting for Philip Pullman's *His Dark Materials* trilogy of books: *Northern Lights* (*The Golden Compass* in the

USA), *The Subtle Knife* and *The Amber Spyglass*. In heroine Lyra Belacqua's alternative universe Oxford is still a city of universities and colleges. However, in her world, the field of science is controlled by the oppressive Magisterium (a thinly veiled representation of severe Catholicism – the technical term Magisterium is used to denote the church's teaching authority), and while some aspects of their science are far in advance of our own, other aspects seem to parallel those of our eighteenth and nineteenth centuries. Also, there are witches and spectres, armoured talking polar bears and any number of other beings that do not exist in our world. One unique aspect of Lyra's universe is that a person's soul exists outside the body and takes the form of a daemon. Daemons can communicate with each other but only with their own partner among humans. To be separated by any great distance causes both of them great pain. When the human is young, their daemon can change shape at will, adopting many different animal forms. However, upon reaching adulthood, the daemon becomes fixed as a single animal, and its form usually gives some indication as to the character of its human – for example, a fox may indicate cunning. Lyra's daemon is called Pantalaimon, or Pan for short, and chooses the form of a pine marten in the final book.

His Dark Materials, which Pullman chose as the overall name for the series, is taken from a verse in *Paradise Lost* by John Milton:

> *The Womb of nature and perhaps her Grave,*
> *Of neither Sea, nor Shore, nor Air, nor Fire,*
> *But all these in thir pregnant causes mix't*
> *Confus'dly, and which thus must ever fight,*
> *Unless th' Almighty Maker them ordain*
> *His dark materials to create more Worlds,*
> *Into this wilde Abyss the warie fiend*
> *Stood on the brink of Hell and look'd a while,*
> *Pondering his Voyage . . .*

Paradise Lost is an epic poem consisting of ten books, although Milton later republished the work divided into twelve. It first appeared in 1667 and the work spans two epic stories: first, the war between Heaven and Hell that saw Lucifer and his defeated armies being banished; second, the tale of Adam and Eve and Original Sin. In both stories the main protagonists lose their place in Paradise. Some scholars see Milton's poem as the first real attempt to reconcile pagan and Christian history. Throughout the work he manages to weave references to classical Greek, Roman and other mythologies into Christian belief. He wrote the poem while completely blind using paid scribes, claiming that he was visited at night by a 'Divine spirit'. He started the poem in 1658 and finished it in 1664. However, publication was delayed due to the Great Plague and the Great Fire of London.

The Great Plague, between 1665 and 1667, killed hundreds of thousands of people. In London alone the Bills of Mortality listed 68,576 plague victims. The true figure is believed to be closer to 100,000 but will probably never be known. But even this was nothing compared to the Black Death pandemic that killed nearly one third (20 million) of Europe's population in the 1300s.

The cause of death in both cases was bubonic plague, and it was a horrible way to die. The victim's skin turned black in patches and inflamed glands (buboes – hence bubonic) grew in the groin, with vomiting, splitting headaches and, in the pneumonic version of the illness, swollen tongues and throats, coughing and rheumy eyes. It must have been agonizing. Because people believed that smells (known as miasmas) were the carriers of disease, they attempted to ward off the illness by dousing themselves in perfume or by holding a posy, or nosegay, of flowers to the face. This, some say, is commemorated in the children's rhyme 'Ring-a-ring o' roses', which, in a macabre way, appears to describe the symptoms of the disease. However, this is almost certainly an urban myth.

According to Professor Ian Munro of Harvard University, who has made a long and in-depth study of the rhyme, the earliest printed version dates from only 1881,[27] some 225 years after the Great Plague, and some 550 years after the Black Death pandemic. Words and phrases can remain underground a long time, but two centuries seems a bit unlikely. Plus, the 1881 version is not so easy to attach to the plague:

> *Ring-a-ring o' roses,*
> *A pocket full of posies,*
> *Hush! hush! hush! hush!*
> *We're all tumbled down*

Munro states:

'This version appears not so much as a story about

---

27 In Kate Greenaway's Mother Goose (1881).

death and disease, but rather about falling asleep after a day of picking flowers.'[28]

Another origin is suggested by the researchers at Quite Interesting Ltd (QI) who, in *The Book of General Ignorance*,[29] state that the first recorded instance of the rhyme was from Massachusetts in 1790. This is still a long way from 1665 ... and a very long way from London.

Also, as many medical books joyfully explain in gruesome detail, the first major symptom of plague is fever and there are generally no respiratory symptoms. Even in its pneumonic form the infection is in the lungs. So coughing, and not sneezing, is the main symptom.

The Random House Dictionary of Popular Proverbs and Sayings states: 'in many cultures it is believed that the soul leaves the body during a sneeze, and God is called on to protect the sneezer from evil spirits at such a vulnerable time'.[30]

This is maybe the origin of the tradition of saying 'Bless you' after someone sneezes. After all, it makes sense to bless someone after they've lost a chunk of

---

28 www.drama.arts.uci.edu/faculty/munro.html.

29 John Lloyd and John Mitchinson (2006) QI/Faber and Faber. www.qi.com.

30 Gregory Y. Titelman, Random House, New York, 1996.

their soul as their head is now a vacuum that could be filled with evil spirits. The blessing allows time for the soul to return home. But how would that work in Lyra's world where the soul is already outside the body? Incidentally, the German word *Gesundheit*, also said often after sneezing, simply means 'Good health!'

Sneezing is a powerful reflex action that involves muscles of the face, head, neck and chest. There is some debate over how fast air is expelled during a sneeze and assertions range from a conservative 100 mph to a claim by the JFK Health World Museum in Barrington, Illinois (Barrington, you may recall, is also the forename of the man who wrote the music for *Inspector Morse*) that a sneeze can go as fast as 630 mph or approximately 85 per cent of the speed of sound.

'Speed of Sound' was the first single to be released from Coldplay's third album *X&Y* and the 1,000,000,000th song to be downloaded from the Apple-owned iTunes Music Store . . . but was famously denied the number one single slot in the UK by the dance mix of 'Axel F' by Crazy Frog.

UK band Coldplay took their name from a collection of poems . . .

Round 29

LET'S HAVE
A WHOPPER

Ron English is a Texan artist and urban 'popagand-ist' who first made a name for himself in the 1980s by altering large-scale advertising posters or substituting them with his own work. Invariably, the messages on his posters and hoardings attacked US government policy, multinational corporations (such as Disney and McDonald's) and harmful products such as caffeine, sugar-rich children's drinks and cigarettes. English also draws upon icons of popular culture for his work and subverts them to get his messages across. Thus, he has painted Mickey Mouse crucified on a mouse trap, an obese Ronald McDonald and grotesque parodies of Apple's 'Think different' campaign posters substituting murderer Charles Manson and Apple nemesis Bill Gates for the usual images of people like Gandhi or Einstein.

Albert Einstein (1879–1955) was born a German non-practising Jew and excelled in the sciences from an early age. There are stories that he was a schoolboy dunce but the truth is that he was a brilliant young student and published his first scientific paper at the age of 15. By 1911 he was a professor of physics at the University of Zurich. He then had a series of positions in universities across Europe and in America. In 1915 he published the work for which he is best known, his *General Theory of Relativity*. Over the years he worked with some of the greatest physicists of all time including Nils Bohr, Satyendra Nath Bose, Werner Heisenberg and Erwin Schrödinger.

When Adolf Hitler came to power in January 1933 Einstein was a guest professor at Princeton University, New Jersey. As the Nazis were forcing all Jewish university professors out of their jobs, Einstein elected to stay in the USA, becoming an American citizen in 1940. In 1939 he sent a letter to President Franklin D. Roosevelt urging him to invest research money in nuclear fission for military purposes, as he feared that the Nazis would be first to develop atomic weapons. Roosevelt agreed and this prompted the Manhattan Project that led ultimately to the creation of the atomic bomb. Einstein, a lifelong pacifist, was not part of the project and in later years regretted his initial involvement.

Manhattan is a borough of New York City and the most densely populated county in the USA. It lies between the East and Hudson Rivers and houses America's main financial district including the Stock Exchange, NASDAQ and, until 11 September 2001, the twin towers of the World Trade Center. The United Nations building is also there.

'Manhattan' derives from the Lenape Indian word *manna-hata*, which means island of many mountains. The first non-native people to settle the area were the Dutch, who named the region New Netherland and established the town of New Amsterdam. And it might have stayed that way had not King Charles II decided to annexe New Netherland in 1664 and make it a part of his new British Empire. The Dutch were allowed to stay and some Dutch place names (Harlem, for example) were retained. Ultimately, the English consolidated their hold on North America and the growing city was renamed New York after the Duke of York, later to be King James II.

The title Duke of York is usually given to the second son of the ruling British monarch. The title has never been passed on by heredity as every holder has either died without male children or has become king. The current holder, Prince Andrew, is no exception as he has two daughters. Therefore the next holder is likely to be Prince Henry (commonly called Harry), second son of Prince Charles and the late Princess Diana.

The title is immortalized in the children's rhyme 'The Grand Old Duke of York' – which shares its tune with the Cornish 'national anthem', 'Trelawny'. There are two candidates for the subject of the song: first, there is Prince Frederick, Duke of York and Albany, second son of King George III and commander-in-chief of the British army during the Napoleonic Wars. The 'hill' may be the town of Cassel in northern France, which rises about 570 feet above the otherwise flat landscape of Flanders. The second candidate is Richard, Duke of York, who in December 1460 was awaiting reinforcements at 'the top of the hill' in Sandal Castle in Wakefield, West Yorkshire. Surrounded by Lancastrian forces outnumbering his own three to one, Richard nevertheless decided to engage the enemy and was killed, along with half his men. Incidentally, this event also gave rise to the popular mnemonic 'Richard of York gave battle in vain' for remembering the sequence of colours of the visible spectrum: red, orange, yellow, green, blue, indigo (if you accept that it exists) and violet.

Violet Beauregarde is a character from the Roald Dahl novel *Charlie and the Chocolate Factory*. She is a world-record-holding chewing gum champion who, because of her bad behaviour, gets turned into a giant blueberry. In the 1971 film version of the book – called *Willy Wonka and the Chocolate Factory* – Willy Wonka mentions a kind of monster called a Vermicious Knid. They are also mentioned in the book (and in *James and the Giant Peach*) and actually make an appearance in the sequel, *Charlie and the Great Glass Elevator*.

Vermicious Knids are a species of shape-shifting alien from the planet Vermes. In their natural form they are huge and egg-shaped and live in the vacuum of space, where they attack spaceships by ramming them with their pointy ends. They are vain creatures and cannot resist showing off. For instance, they can only spell one word – scram – and will form themselves into the shape of the word at every opportunity. Willy Wonka states that they have wiped out many other alien species.

Vermicious is a real word and means worm-like. 'Knid', meanwhile, may have been inspired by *Cni-*

daria, the family of animals that includes jellyfish and coral. *Cnidaria* in turn derives from *cnidos*, the Greek word for stinging nettle.

Nettles contain a number of mild poisons: histamine to irritate the skin, acetylcholine to bring on a burning sensation and serotonin to increase the effects of both. Serotonin is a neurotransmitter and in the central nervous system is involved in the regulation of sleep, body temperature, sexuality, mood and appetite.

Low levels of serotonin can lead to clinical depression and other disorders. Excessively high levels of serotonin can have toxic and potentially fatal effects, and regular use of such drugs as MDMA (Ecstasy) can contribute to this.

There is also a strong body of scientific opinion which asserts that enhanced – but not dangerous – levels of serotonin are responsible for feelings of enlightenment and spirituality. Prince Siddhartha Gautama, the spiritual teacher and founder of Buddhism, found enlightenment under the Bodhi Tree, which is a sacred fig (*Ficus religiosa*). Figs are known to be rich in serotonin.

The largest fig tree in the world (although the record seems to be disputed, with claimants in Santa Barbara, California and Cairns, Australia) can be found in the Royal Botanical Gardens in Kandy, Sri Lanka's second city. This Javan fig tree (*Ficus benjamina*) covers a staggering area of 1900 square yards. Kandy is also where you will find the Temple of the Tooth – Sri Dalada Maligaw – where a fragment of one of the Buddha's teeth is kept. Around the temple and all over Sri Lanka are bell-shaped Buddhist temples called *dagoba*s.

Dagobah is the name of the swamp planet chosen for his exile by the Jedi master Yoda in the *Star Wars* films. Following the overthrow of the Republic and the destruction of the Jedi Order, Yoda and his colleagues needed to hide, regroup and grow stronger. Obi-Wan Kenobi chose the desert planet of Tatooine in order to watch over the child Luke Skywalker (George Lucas named this planet after Tataouine in Tunisia – one of the real locations used during filming). Many of the place and character names in *Star Wars* can be traced back to terrestrial origins in myth and history. Others are simply puns or homages. Examples include the aquatic-looking Mon Calamari race (which translates as 'my squid') and Jabba the Hutt's skiff guards Klaatu, Barada and Nikto. These were the three words spoken by Michael Rennie's alien character (called Klaatu) in the 1951 science fiction classic *The Day the Earth Stood Still*. The phrase was also used by Ash (Bruce Campbell) to open the Necronomicon in the movie *Army of Darkness*.

The *Necronomicon* is a fictional book invented by the writer H. P. Lovecraft (1890–1937). Lovecraft's invention was essentially the Bible's 'evil twin' and he constructed an elaborate history for it. The book was originally known as *Al Aʒif* and written by a half-crazed Arabic worshipper of the 'Old Ones' called Abdul Alhazred, who died in AD 738. The book was later translated into Latin by one Olaus Wormius sometime around 1334[31] and English by Elizabethan magician John Dee (1527–1609).

The name was also used for the first major book of work by Swiss surrealist painter Hans Ruedi Giger. *H. R. Giger's Necronomicon* (1977) was banned from many bookshops upon its release because of the disturbing content. Among the images within are baby-headed condoms, landscapes apparently made of festering meat, amputees, rotting bodies and sexual organs (he was the subject of an obscenity lawsuit at one point). His work has an almost photorealistic 3-D quality at times, which adds to the sense of unease. A common

---

31 There was a real Olaus Wormius but he lived 1599–1624.

feature is the idea of flesh and technology fusing together. Giger calls the creatures in his paintings biomechanoids and it was one such creature that inspired the producers of the 1979 film *Alien* to ask Giger to design all of the alien aspects – creatures, spaceships and planets – for the film. Giger won an Oscar for his work in 1980. He went on to design aliens and buildings for the films *Species* and *Dune*. He also designed a number of LP covers including *Koo Koo* for Debbie Harry and *Brain Salad Surgery* for Emerson, Lake and Palmer.

ELP, as they were known, were one of the giants of progressive rock. Prog rock has always been difficult to categorize. There are some common themes however: expert musicianship; the use of 'light and dark' tracks that feature juxtapositions of loud and fast music with calm, melodic interludes; and concept tracks or albums where all of the music fits into an overall theme or story. Another common feature is long tracks broken into sections or movements, much like a symphony. Prog extends across a wide range of musical genres such as jazz, metal, neo-classical, folk and so-called new age music.

One of the most successful new age artists of recent

years is Medwyn Goodall. A multi-instrumentalist, he has written and recorded nearly 150 albums and sold more than two million copies worldwide. He lives in Cornwall, where he runs his own recording studio. Many of the covers for his early albums were painted by St Ives-based new age visionary artist Keith English. English claims that his life was turned around by a spirit guide called Khutumi, who taught him to explore his spiritual and metaphysical self. English has never looked back and his paintings are now collectors' items.

Another artist called English (also based in Cornwall) is armourer Terry English. He has made swords, suits of armour and other metallic outfits for many exhibitions and feature films. These include *Gladiator*, the space marines' armour in *Aliens* (fighting against Giger's aliens), Arnold Swarzenegger's Mr Freeze outfit in *Batman and Robin* and the knights' armour in *Excalibur* and *King Arthur*.

Terry and Keith are not related but the surname does seem popular within the artist community: there is a Michael English, who designed posters for Pink Floyd and others during the 1960s and '70s. Much of his work was collected in a book published by Paper

Tiger and called *3D Eye*. And there is a US artist called Ron English.

Ron English is a Texan artist and urban . . .

Round 30

I'D LIKE TO THANK . . .

My name is Stevyn Colgan and this is the final complete Round. I'd like to use it to thank all those people – friends, family and strangers – who have helped me create this book. I can't possibly include everyone I could thank (or everyone who has inspired me) so I'll have to make do with a generic 'Thank you!' to you all. However, certain people require extra-special thanks for providing facts and for acting as sounding boards. I'll start with Huw Williams. No one could have been more supportive and helpful to me as I pulled this monster together. Thanks, Huw! We've known each other since we were kids, growing up together in Helston, Cornwall.

Helston is the home of the world-famous Furry Dance, which takes place on Flora Day on 8 May every year. During the day a whole series of dances takes place following ancient prescribed routes which take the dancers along certain streets and through people's houses, gardens and shops. The tune performed during the dances is the 'Helston Floral Dance', which was popularized firstly by the Brighouse and Rastrick Brass Band and then by TV and radio personality Terry Wogan in 1978.

Terry Wogan is a popular Irish broadcaster who regularly appears on BBC radio and television. The second person I'd like to thank is also Irish – my great friend, artist James Murphy. Thanks, Murph!

Wogan was born in Limerick, Ireland, but took dual Irish/British nationality so that he could accept an honorary knighthood from the Queen. He once held the world record for the longest successful televised golf putt – 33 yards – which he achieved in a pro-celebrity tournament at Gleneagles. TV golf commentator Peter Alliss described it as 'the most remarkable shot I've ever seen in my life'.

Wogan is also famous for having fallen on his backside during the live broadcast of the very first episode of his eponymously named BBC chat show in 1985 . . . much to the amusement of guest Elton John.

Elton John is a supporter of Watford Football Club and, until 2002, the club's director and chairman. Watford in Hertfordshire is very close to where my third and fourth thankees live, father and son sculptors and prosthetists David and Arran Gavin. Cheers, lads! I first met Dave through my sculptor friend John Coppinger, who's given me loads of great facts and stories. Thanks, John! John has worked on many feature films and TV series and is the man who sculpted Jabba the Hutt for *Star Wars Episode 6 – The Return of the Jedi.*

Return of the Jedi saw Alec Guinness reprise his role as Obi-Wan Kenobi. He featured in all three of the first trilogy of *Star Wars* films (ultimately Episodes 4, 5 and 6) but only appeared to any great degree in the first film. Famously, Guinness was not enamoured of his part in the *Star Wars* saga – which he regarded as a children's story and a bit silly – and some claim that he persuaded George Lucas to have Obi-Wan killed off. Guinness also refused to attend *Star Wars* conventions or to reply to fan mail. In later years his views mellowed and he is quoted as saying, 'I might never have been heard of again if it hadn't been for *Star Wars.*' This seems unlikely as Guinness was an extremely versatile and professional actor with a stunning CV. He was so professional that when filming *Star Wars* he was spotted rolling around in the Tunisian dust before shooting as he believed Obi-Wan

Kenobi's robes were too clean. That certainly wouldn't have pleased my good friend Debbie Hodson who is very possibly obsessive-compulsive when it comes to cleaning. Thanks for listening to my ranting over the years, Debs!

I was told by my film, TV and comics journalist chum Joel Meadows of *Tripwire* magazine – another man with a great capacity for facts and stories (Ta, mate!) – that Guinness's phone number at his home in Hampshire was just one digit different to the number for the local butchers, and that Guinness received a constant stream of calls from people ordering meat. After some years he got fed up with explaining that they had the wrong number and amused himself instead by taking their orders, and then telling them off for making bad choices or for buying cheap cuts. He would then pass the orders on to the butcher.

Butchery and taxidermy used to go hand in hand at one time, with edible meat being taken from hunted animals and the pelt and other parts used for clothing or to mount the dead animal as a trophy. Taxidermy, in the modern artistic and scientific sense of the word, can be traced back to the work of several pioneers including the brilliantly named Ole Worm of Denmark (1588–1655). But the modern art was developed in the nineteenth and twentieth centuries by people like Carl E. Akeley, James L. Clark, William T. Hornaday, Coleman Jonas, Fredrick and William Kaempfer, and Leon Pray.

The first taxidermist I ever met was a chap called Roy Hale. His son Chris has been a close friend of mine for over 25 years and someone I've turned to time and time again when I've needed to test out ideas. Thanks, Chris! His dad was at one time the chief taxidermist and model maker at London's famous Natural History Museum. Many of Roy's ex-staff (including the aforementioned John Coppinger) now work as model makers, sculptors and special effects technicians for companies like Industrial Light and Magic, Crawley Creatures and Jim Henson's Creature Workshop. I never met Jim Henson but I do know a Neil Henson (no relation) and I'd like to thank him, Geoff Williams, Stewart Levy, Colin Riley, Jane Farmery, Julia Borwick and a brace of Pauls – Paul King and Paul Scott. They have nothing to do with museums or Muppets but I used to work with them all and they always supported my creative efforts and listened to my mad ideas. Thanks, guys! Right, back to the Natural History Museum.

The Natural History Museum in London's Exhibition Road is an extraordinary building. One of the grand Victorian museums of the nineteenth century, it was designed by Alfred Waterhouse. The building is Gothic in style and sports dramatic arches and towers. And everywhere you look the building is ornamented inside and out with terracotta gargoyles and sculptures of animals and plants. But we very nearly didn't get the museum we see today. The 1862 International Exhibition Building – once described as the ugliest building in London – previously stood on the site and, ironically, its architect, Captain Francis Fowke, was chosen to design the new museum. However, Fowke died suddenly just after being awarded the contract and Waterhouse got the job by default. Waterhouse's masterpiece opened to the public on Easter Monday 1881.

Easter, which we associate today with Christianity (most notably the resurrection of Christ and Lent), actually takes its name from a pagan Anglo-Saxon goddess called Eostre. At least, that was the claim made by the 'father of English history', the Venerable Bede (AD 672–735), in his book *De Tempore Ratione* (On the Reckoning of Time). Bede hailed from Northumbria, also the home county of my artist friend Jan 'Boris' Szymczuk, to whom I also owe thanks. Cheers,

Boris! His surname is Polish and is pronounced 'Shim-shook'. Another friend with a Polish name I must say thanks to is Ed Jedrzejczak. I've known him for years but I still no idea how his surname is pronounced. And he won't tell me. It's become a kind of game (I suspect he doesn't know either). His partner's name is much easier − Teresa Hancock − and she's been a great mate too, as have Liz and Simon Fraser and Steve Carroll. Thanks, guys!

Further proof of its pagan origins can be found in the way that the date of Easter is calculated. Easter Sunday can fall on any one of 35 dates between 22 March and 25 April but is always on the first Sunday following the first ecclesiastical full Moon that occurs on or after the day of the vernal equinox (which was set by the Church as 21st March). The ecclesiastical full Moon (which is determined by a set of tables drawn up in 1582) generally ties in with the astronomical new Moon but can vary slightly. The main point to stress is that the date of Easter is set by the Moon, and pagan calendars revolved around the Moon. Christianity adopted a solar calendar instead. And then there's the name of course. Many linguists agree that Eostre and Ostara (from which we get Easter) are derived from the Old Teutonic root *aew-s*, which means 'to illuminate, especially of daybreak'. The word is also closely related to *(a)wes-ter*, meaning dawn servant, and *austrón*, meaning dawn.

All of which brings me to my fantastic wife Dawn and my kids Sarah, Kerys and Liam, whom I have to thank for leaving me alone when I needed to concentrate. And I cannot leave my family without mention of my brother Jake, who has always been there for me – even at the most ridiculous and unsociable hours – when I've needed advice or a sympathetic ear. And then there's my mum Meg and my late father Myghal. Dad was a major influence in my life, encouraging me to search constantly for knowledge and to find ways to improve myself. He also passed on to me via his DNA a flair for art, music and creativity. At this point I should also thank the late Douglas Adams, whose initials were D.N.A., for kind words and inspiration. Even though I only met him once, he was very enthusiastic about my writing and it spurred me on. Dad would have enjoyed this book as he was a veritable magpie when it came to trivia and interesting facts. He was also a writer and a passionate Cornishman, who used the Cornish spelling of his name Michael (Myghal) as his nom de plume. It was therefore only right that when I decided to write professionally (and sharing the same passion for my home county), I adopted the Cornish spelling of Stephen: Stevyn.

Another Stephen that I must thank before I go is Stephen Fry – actor, raconteur, writer and national treasure. He championed this book and led me to John Mitchinson and John Lloyd of QI Ltd, who were invaluable in focusing my efforts. Thanks also to the many QI Elves in the various forums and discussion groups at www.qi.com for airing their views, correcting my mistakes and suggesting links. It was due to these guys, the tireless work of my dapper agent, Ben Mason, my brilliant editor, Jon Butler, and Sandra Taylor and Amy Lines at Pan Macmillan, that this book became possible. Thanks, chaps!

And so, with an army of friends and family and elves behind me, and armed with a suitable title for the book, I adopted a Cornish pen name for myself and set to work.

My name is Stevyn Colgan and . . .

The joined-up index

Fleming – Eugène Delacroix – *Les Misérables* – Virginia – Elizabeth I – *Bessie* – MTR5 robot – John Dee – British Empire – James Bond

Round 7   *The Flintstones* – *Scooby Doo* – Frank Sinatra – *Roger Rabbit* – Hammerspace – Superman – Seinfeld – Amex – Wells Fargo – Oscars – Halle Berry – *The Flintstones*

Round 8   Bees – Barbie – Harley-Davidson – Tony Blair – George Orwell – Room 101 – Stasi – Christopher Marlowe – Shakespeare – Francis Bacon – binary – ABC – cancer – periwinkle – pollination – bees

Round 9   'Chopsticks' – deforestation – Oxfam – Coldplay – BST – Chronos – French opera – Arthur de Lulli – 'Chopsticks'

Round 10   UFO – B2 bomber – E101 – alimentary canal – elementary – Sherlock Holmes – *Star Trek* – *Thunderbirds* – Gerry Anderson – UFO

Round 11   The avocado – giant sloth – Christopher Columbus – Leif Ericson – *The High Chaparral* – Cochise – Indians – lignum vitae – Merlin – red wine – berries – the avocado

Round 12   Roald Dahl – Peaches Geldof – Paula Yates – Hughie Green – Freddie Starr – Grand

National – Red Rum – Boston Strangler –
The Stranglers – Roald Dahl

Round 13 *The Wizard of Oz* – duels – dysentery –
Klingerman – tapeworms – Atkins – autopsies
– drinking water – angina – L. Frank Baum –
The Wizard of Oz

Round 14 Taipei 101 – Gustave Eiffel – Lady Liberty –
Planet of the Apes – Hannibal Lecter – *The A-
Team* – Audrey Hepburn – Edward III –
Prince Charles – Romania – Vlad the Impaler
– St Bartholomew – tanning – *101 Dalmatians*
– Taipei 101

Round 15 Roger Dean – Charles Dickens – Revd Robert
Hawker – National Trust – yellow fever –
Mosquito – Bristol Blenheim – Jupiter –
Roger Dean

Round 16 The Madagascar Plan – the Holocaust – IBM
– HAL – acronyms – Danny Wallace – Frat
Pack – Wright Brothers – chard – sugar beet
– the Madagascar Plan

Round 17 Kenning – beer – the armadillo – leprosy –
Robert the Bruce – Mackintosh – Apple –
iPod – bushels – Kenning

Round 18 Margaret Rutherford – *Mr Benn* – Putney –
David Copperfield – Great Wall of China –

Boxer Rebellion – Simon and Garfunkel – B52 bomber – nuclear fission – Ernest Rutherford – Margaret Rutherford

Round 19 Chicken hypnosis – Iggy Pop – *Cry Baby* – Patty Hearst – Stockholm syndrome – Muse – the 'face on Mars' – the Sphinx – Mighty Morphin Power Rangers – chicken hypnosis

Round 20 The Green Man – Batman – Robin Hood – King John – Douglas Fairbanks – Charlie Chaplin – Laurel and Hardy – Llanfairpwllgwyngyllgogerychwyrndrobwllllantisiliogogogoch – witch hazel – dowsing – MDMA – XTC – the Green Man

Round 21 The Asteroid Belt – Ceres – Eris – Xena – Hercules – Olympus Mons – the Holy Prepuce – cloning – Dolly the sheep – Dolly Parton – ISR – IAU – the Asteroid Belt

Round 22 *Torchwood* – *Dr Who* – Peter Cushing – Christopher Lee – Strategic Defence Initiative – Pebbles Flintstone – Havering – the Proclaimers – *Shrek* – greetings cards – Hallmark – crowns – the Magi – *Torchwood*

Round 23 Chickens – CPR – *Cardiac Arrest* – Murray Mints – Stargazers – Galileo – *Mary Celeste* – Amazons – Amazonsaurus – talpids – chickens

Round 24   Kylie Minogue – Traci Lords – Hawaii – the Earl of Sandwich – John Wilkes – the Hellfire Club – baboons – flange – Rowan Atkinson – Natalie Imbruglia – *Neighbours* – Kylie Minogue

Round 25   Cats – poachers – Robin Hood – Clive Mantle – *The Vicar of Dibley* – Richard Curtis – Douglas Adams – Probability – Schrödinger's Cat – cats

Round 26   Feeder – Buck Rogers – Glen A. Larson – Martin Caidin – *The Six Million Dollar Man* – *Magnum P.I.* – *Hawaii Five-O* – *The A-Team* – *Breakfast at Tiffany's* – Wilfred Hyde White – *Battlestar Galactica* – Feeder

Round 27   Starfish – hermaphrodites – molly houses – Super Guppy – beluga – narwhal – Feejee Mermaids – *Family Guy* – clams – starfish

Round 28   Coldplay – Baudot code – Morse code – *Inspector Morse* – Oxford – *His Dark Materials* – *Paradise Lost* – bubonic plague – sneezing – Coldplay

Round 29   Ron English – Albert Einstein – Manhattan – Duke of York – violet – Vermicious Knids – nettles – serotonin – Buddha – fig trees – Dagobah – *Necronomicon* – H. R. Giger –

prog rock – new age music – Medwyn
Goodall – Keith English – Terry English –
Ron English

Round 30 Me – Helston – Terry Wogan – Watford –
Alec Guinness – butchery and taxidermy –
Natural History Museum – the Venerable Bede
– Easter – And a big thank you to all my
friends and family who helped me create this
book.

The great big joined-up index

Now here's the thing . . .

After I'd completed my 30 Rounds, I felt that I had enough material to consider publishing a book. So I sent a copy to some of my friends for their views – they're all listed in Round 30. They were, I'm pleased to say, overwhelmingly positive, but then I met Huw for a few beers and asked for his opinion.

'Very good,' he said. 'But if everything really can be connected to everything else, surely you could link all 30 Rounds to each other? Then I'd be really impressed.'

Always up for a challenge, I set out to do just that. I already knew that certain facts within the various Rounds could be connected to facts in other Rounds. I just hadn't realized quite how many could be connected.

So here, for your entertainment, is the 'Great big joined-up index'.

It made my brain hurt.

Round 1 mentions *The Wizard of Oz* and can therefore be linked to *Round 13* (L. Frank Baum's coat). *Round 1* also links to *Round 4* by way of Irvine Walsh. Sir Isaac Newton appears here and in *Round 18* and his colour indigo in *Round 29*. Alchemy is mentioned here and in *Round 8*. Mars looms here as it does in *Rounds 4, 19* and *21*. Pink Floyd play here and in *Rounds 2* and *29*. The number seven appears here and in *Round 6* by way of 007. Shakespeare appears here and in *Round 8*.

Round 2 mentions the Sex Pistols, as does *Round 20*. And Johnny Rotten's 'I Hate Pink Floyd' T-shirt links him to *Rounds 1* and *29*. Indiana Jones makes a heroic appearance here and in *Rounds 13* and *26*. Morse code is used here and in *Round 28*.

Round 3 has chickens in it and so do *Rounds 19* and *23*. Lent links this Round to *Round 30*. Vermicious mealworms burrow here and in *Round 29*. Chronos and Zeus/Jupiter appear here and in *Rounds 4, 9, 15* and *21*.

Round 4 links to *Round 1* via mention of Irvine Walsh. It also links to Frank Sinatra via *Rounds 5, 7* and *21*. And the song 'My Way' links *Round 4* to *Round 2*. Oscars are also awarded in *Rounds 7, 14* and *21*. *Star Wars* and Alec Guinness link to *Rounds 29* and *30*. Mars can be observed here and in *Rounds 1, 19* and *21*. Chronos and Zeus/Jupiter appear here and in *Rounds 3, 9, 15* and *21*.

Round 5, as already mentioned, links to *Rounds 4, 7* and *21* by way of Frank Sinatra. But it also links to *Round 6* because of JFK and to *Round 12* by way of *Opportunity Knocks*.

Lobotomies link this Round to *Round 14*. And Liberty – the statue and character – stands proudly here and in *Rounds 6*, *14*, *18* and *20*, making Lady Liberty a very popular lady. David Bowie stars here and in *Rounds 4* and *19*.

Round 6 can be linked to *Rounds 7*, *10* and *22* by *Dr Who* and to *Round 18* by Simon and Garfunkel. JFK links it back to *Round 5*. *Looney Tunes* are mentioned here and in *Rounds 7* and *26*. James Bond is spying here and in *Rounds 10*, *24* and *25* and Sean Connery is also mentioned in *Round 25*. The word daemon appears here and in *Round 28*. John Dee also materializes in *Round 29* and astrology features here and in *Rounds 22*, *23* and *27*. His boss Queen Elizabeth I appears here and in *Round 8*. Swiss is also mentioned in *Round 29*. *Round 6* features 007, a number dealt with in some detail in *Round 1*. Christopher Lee menaces us here and in *Rounds 22* and *29*.

Round 7 links Frank Sinatra to *Rounds 4*, *5* and *21*. *The Flintstones* are also mentioned in *Rounds 18* and *22*. Razzies are passed out here and in *Round 18*. The Oscar (Academy Award) is mentioned in *Rounds 4*, *14* and *21*. *Round 7* mentions *Looney Tunes* (also mentioned in *Rounds 6* and *26*) and Hanna-Barbera ... who made the original *Tom and Jerry* cartoons (*Round 6*). *Dr Who* materializes here and in *Rounds 6*, *10* and *22*. Jim Carrey stars here and in *Round 16*.

Round 8 provides the first appearance of the number 101, which subsequently appears in *Rounds 10*, *14* and *16*. Madagascar is mentioned in *Rounds 8* and *16*. Alchemy appears here and in *Round 1*. Elizabeth I reigns supreme here and in *Round 6*. And because *Round 8* deals with spies, it could possibly be linked to all of the James Bond references in *Rounds 6, 10, 24* and *25*. Shakespeare appears here and in *Round 1*.

Round 9 links Jupiter/Zeus to *Rounds 3, 4, 15* and *21*. It also links Coldplay to *Round 28*.

Round 10 and *Round 18* both describe the B2 stealth bomber. *Opportunity Knocks* and lobotomies can be linked back to *Round 5*. *Dr Who* warps into this Round and *Rounds 6, 7* and *22*. The number 101 appears here as it does in *Rounds 8, 14* and *16*. *Star Trek* transports this Round to *Round 21*. James Bond sidles his way in here and in *Rounds 6, 24* and *25*.

Round 11 features Merlin in the form of a wizard and *Round 15* as an engine. It also mentions Native American Indians, as does *Round 29*. And berries – such as blueberries – roll in here and in *Round 29*.

Round 12 links the Green Man to *Round 20* and Roald Dahl to *Round 29*.

Round 13 links to *Round 1* and *The Wizard of Oz*. Indiana Jones appears here and in *Rounds 2* and *26*.

Round 14 and *Round 15* both mention Woodstock, Blenheim Palace and David Copperfield. Lady Liberty can be seen here and in *Rounds 5, 6, 18* and *20*. Oscars link this Round to

Rounds *4*, *7* and *21*. The number 101 appears here and in *Rounds* *8*, *10* and *16*. Audrey Hepburn and the A-Team join forces to link this Round to *Round* *26*. Prince Charles also appears in *Round* *29*.

Round *15* links Roger Dean to *Round* *2* as he designed the first ever Virgin logo, and to Yes and Rick Wakeman (*Round* *4*) as he designed album covers for them. Oh, and to *Rounds* *1* and *2* as he did the cover for *The Orchestral Pink Floyd*. Oh, and to Charles Dickens (*18*) as he did covers for the band Uriah Heep. Charles Dickens links *Round* *15* to *Round* *18*. Blenheim Palace, Woodstock and David Copperfield are all mentioned in *Round* *14* too. *Round* *15* mentions Merlin as does *Round* *11*. Jupiter/Zeus links back to *Rounds* *3*, *4*, *9* and *21* and Trelawny to *Round* *29* (and maybe *30*). *Round* *15* also mentions High Wycombe as does *Round* *24*.

Round *16* mentions acronyms and IBM; so does *Round* *17*. Madagascar links *Round* *16* back to *Round* *8*. *Round* *16* features Nazis as does *Round* *29*. And there's yet another mention of the number 101 already mentioned in *Rounds* *8*, *10* and *14*. Jews appear in this Round and in *Rounds* *21* and *29*. Jim Carrey has us laughing here and in *Round* *7*.

Round *17* links back to *16* as just described (Acronyms and IBM). It also links to *Rounds* *28* and *29* by way of Apple – as fruit, computers and rock star children.

Round *18* links to *Rounds* *7* and *22* by mention of *The Flintstones* and to *Round* *7* by way of the Razzie awards.

The great big joined-up index

Charles Dickens scribbles here and in *Round 15*. The B2 bomber soars here and over *Round 10*. The Statue of Liberty links *Round 18* to *Rounds 5, 6, 14* and *20*. Simon and Garfunkel link back to *Round 6*. Sir Isaac Newton makes an appearance in this Round and *Round 1*. And the atom bomb explodes here and in *Round 29*.

Round 19 links David Bowie to *Round 4* and chickens to *Rounds 3* and *23*. Mars links this Round to *Rounds 1, 4* and *21* and Traci Lords to *Round 24*.

Round 20 features the Sex Pistols, last seen in *Round 2*. Lady Liberty also appears as she does in *5, 6, 14* and *18*. Batman and Robin are on patrol here and in *Round 29*. *Round 20*'s Green Man is also mentioned in *Round 12*. Laurel and Hardy are fooling around here and in *Round 22*. Robin Hood swings in here and in *Round 25*. Ecstasy features here and in *Round 29*.

Round 21 mentions Mars as do *Rounds 1, 19* (and *4* if you count 'Life on Mars'). The Moon features prominently and does form part of the title of Pink Floyd's *Dark Side of the Moon* album mentioned in *Round 1*. Pluto (planet) is mentioned while Pluto (dog) appears in *Round 7*. Dwarf planets feature in this Round while dwarfs (or dwarves) are discussed in *Round 1*. Jesus appears here and in *Round 22*. Zeus is mentioned as the father of Hercules and appears in *Rounds 3, 4, 9* and *15*. The Oscars are given out here and in *Rounds 4, 7* and *14*. *Round 27* mentions asteroids and astronomy, both featured here. Frank Sinatra croons here and in *Rounds* *4*, *5* and *7*. *Star Trek* links to *Round* *10*. Finally, Jews feature here and in *Rounds* *16* and *29*.

Round *22* mentions *Dr Who* as do *Rounds* *6*, *7* and *10*. It also links to *Round* *20* by reference to Laurel and Hardy. Jesus features here and in *Round* *21*. Astrology is also consulted in *Rounds* *6*, *23* and *27*. Roald Dahl appears here and in *Rounds* *12* and *29*. Christopher Lee stars in a film mentioned in *Rounds* *6* and *29*.

Round *23* links chickens to *Rounds* *3* and *19*. It also links by way of astrology to *22* and *27* and possibly to John Dee in *Rounds* *6* and *29*.

Round *24* features Traci Lords, as does *Round* *19*. It also mentions the James Bond (also found in *Rounds* *6*, *10* and 25) film *Never Say Never Again* as does *Round* *6*. *Hawaii Five-O* is catching the bad guys here and again in *Round* *26*. Captain Cook sails by here and in *Round* *28*. High Wycombe pops up here and in *Round* *15*.

Round *25* features Robin Hood, who last appeared in *Round* *20*. It also mentions Sean Connery as does *Round* *6*. James Bond too appears here and in *Rounds* *6*, *10* and *24*. Erwin Schrödinger appears here and in *Round* *29*.

Round *26* links both the A-Team and Audrey Hepburn to *Round* *14*. Mention of *Looney Tunes* links this also to *Round* *6* and *Round* *7*. Hawaii is mentioned here as it is in *Round*

24. And Indiana Jones is here (Hoorah!) as he is in *Rounds* *2* and *13*.

Round 27 is attached to *Round 28* by mention of starfish. It also links to *Round 21* by mention of asteroids and to *Rounds 6*, *22* and *23* because of astrology and astronomy.

Round 28 links to *Round 24* by mention of Captain Cook. It also links to *27*, which features starfish. There is a tentative link to *Round 6* through the word daemon and a surer one to *Round 9* because of the band Coldplay. There is also a link to *Rounds 17* and *29* via Apple. This Round mentions Morse code as does *Round 2*.

Round 29 mentions Apple as do *Rounds 17* and *28*. Erwin Schrödinger is let out of the box here and in *Round 25* and the atom bomb is set off here and in *Round 18*. Nazis goose-step their way through this Round to *Round 16* and Jews link us to *Rounds 16* and *21*. Native American Indians are settled here and in *Round 11* and indigo features here and in *Round 1*. Mention of the song 'Trelawny' links with *Round 15* (and possibly *30*). Prince Charles makes an appearance here and also in *Round 14*. Roald Dahl is present here and in *Rounds 12* and *22*. *Charlie and the Chocolate Factory* features Christopher Lee, who was mentioned in *Rounds 6* and *22*. And berries (such as blueberries) appear in *Round 11*. Vermicious mealworms wiggle in *Round 3* and the term is explained in this Round. Ecstasy is here in this Round and *Round 20*. *Star Wars* makes another appearance here as it does in *Rounds 4* and *30*. John Dee links to *Round 6*. Swiss things are mentioned here and in *Round 6* and Keith and Terry English link from here to mentions of Cornwall in *Rounds 15* and *30*. Pink Floyd play their farewell show here (previously in *Rounds 1* and *2*). And Batman and Robin swing in here and in *Round 20*.

Round 30 allows me to mention all those people I have to thank for helping me create this book. There are also some links to other Rounds. *Star Wars* and Alec Guinness are both mentioned here and in *Rounds 4* and *29*. Lent features here and in *Round 3*. And you could, if you really wanted to, link my passion for Cornwall with that most Cornish of songs, 'Trelawny', mentioned in *Rounds 15* and *29*. Maybe.

So there you go.

I am happy to admit that I may have missed some connections. If I have, send them to me at mail@stevecolgan. com.

Alternatively, I could have used the Asteroid Belt (as described in *Round 21*) as my Great big joined-up index. After all, a circle of rocks with a circumference of over 600 million miles is pretty big and many of those rocks are named after people, places and objects that have appeared in this book. For instance, asteroid number 1537 is called Transylvania and 2309 is Mr Spock. Others include 2598 Merlin, 3325 TARDIS, 3846 Hazel, 4238 Audrey (Hepburn), 7707 Yes, 9000 HAL (after HAL9000), 9007 James Bond, 9777 *Enterprise* (from *Star Trek*), 11020 Orwell, 11246 Orville Wright, 11247 Wilbur Wright, 12820 Robin Williams, 13070 Sean Connery and the twins 2865 and 2866 Laurel and

Hardy. There's an Oldfield (after Mike) and a Dickens and a Sinatra and . . .

I could go on and on. But I won't.

An interesting and serendipitous thing happened to me a couple of years ago . . .